The F.A. Guide to Training and Coaching

ALLEN WADE

The F.A. Guide to Training and Coaching

Published on behalf of
THE FOOTBALL ASSOCIATION

HEINEMANN : LONDON

William Heinemann Ltd

LONDON MELBOURNE TORONTO

JOHANNESBURG AUCKLAND

First published 1967
Reprinted 1970
© THE FOOTBALL ASSOCIATION 1967

Printed in Great Britain by
GILMOUR & DEAN LTD., Hamilton and London

Contents

Photographic illustrations in this book were supplied by Ken Walker of Knightway Studios.

Introduction

There are, reputedly, two stages through which worthwhile ideas must pass before they are accepted. In the first stage they are ignored, in the second, ridiculed. Coaching has passed through these stages and is now accepted as a necessary process in the education and development of more skilful players at all levels. Indeed, if this were not so, the whole process of education from early school years to university level could be viewed with doubts and reservations.

A coach's aim is to find the most economical way of causing a player to become a better player in the widest possible sense. This improvement may relate to the player's understanding of the game or to the development of his technique. More likely it concerns a combination of both: indeed these two aspects of a player's capabilities must be interdependent.

In the past, coaching was ignored because the reservoirs of so-called natural talent seemed limitless. It was subsequently ridiculed, probably because some players, eminent in their time, had not been taught, so it was assumed that no-one could be taught. Had this belief prevailed in the musical field, the development of great instrumentalists would surely have been under a handicap.

This book has been written to present the experience of The Football Association over the years in the fields of coaching and training. The knowledge gained has been, and will continue to be, tested and tried, as new ideas emerge and changes occur. The main purpose of the book is not to provide categorical answers or suggest cut-and-dried methods; answers and methods are not so easily arrived at. Its purpose is to present ideas and principles which will require coaches to think. They, in turn, must provoke thought and enquiry among their players. Unthinking coaches and players mean, ultimately, stagnation in the game. Stagnation produces complacency and this must never again be permitted to occur in this country.

A.W.

Acknowledgements

The Football Association depends upon the unselfish and often unsparing efforts of a great many people for the success of its instructional work. The coaching scheme is the result of the intelligence, skill, and football 'know how' of men from all the different levels at which the game is played. To a great extent this book is an attempt to sum up their experience and, as a consequence, my sincere thanks are given to everyone who has contributed to the development of coaching in this country. In particular, my thanks are due to the Staff Coaches of The Football Association. These are the men who are responsible for the National Coaching Courses; men who have provided and who continue to provide so much inspiration in the cause of skilful football.

The preparation of this book would have been considerably hindered without the cheerful effort lavished upon it by my secretary, Joan Pritchard. To her and to the many others who have assisted me, may I express my gratitude.

PART I

Principles, Systems, and Tactics

1 Principles of Team Play

One of the many reasons why Association Football is attractive both to players and spectators is its freedom of movement. Attack and defence flow naturally into each other and players can be almost completely unrestricted in their movements on the field of play. The game, then, is basically a free game, but, as in all team games, the aim of a team must be to win the match. This inevitably means the co-ordination of eleven individual efforts into a combined team effort which demands some planning and hence a certain amount of restriction. The planning must be aimed at making the best of each individual's abilities; the restriction involves the calculation of chance, which is an inherent part of the game. It would be ridiculous, for example, to encourage eight players to adopt major attacking roles in order to secure goals if this policy resulted in the opposing team scoring more goals and, therefore, winning the match.

There are three principal phases of the game:

1. Attack
2. Defence
3. Preparation or mid-field play

In the third phase neither team has established a complete domination of play, but is involved in re-organization before making an attack or building up its defence.

So far no mention has been made of positions although it is quite clear that certain positions vary in their requirements so far as players are concerned. We, in England, see our teams line up at the kick-off in what is known as the pyramid formation (*fig.* 1).

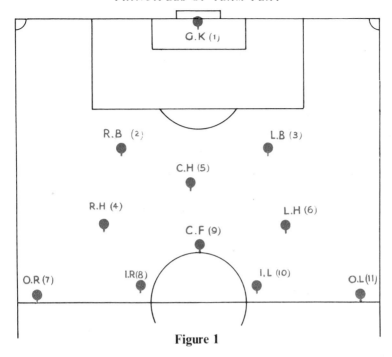

Figure 1

During recent years, however, changes have taken place in this structure. The stopper centre-half has been recognized for what he is, a third full-back, and in some countries this is shown both in the opening formation and in the numbering of players (*fig.* 2).

Other countries have adopted a system where there are four 'backs', two 'half-backs' and four 'forwards'. A logical line-up and system of numbering under these circumstances might be that shown in *fig.* 3.

All that this serves to emphasize is that the game is not played by numbers; indeed, the only real significance of numbers is that they serve to identify players in match programmes. Unfortunately, this is not always the case in practice; crowds are often bewildered when players in a team appear to be occupying positions bearing no relation to the numbers on their shirts.

There are have been considerable changes in the systems of play developed over the years, and certainly in the tactical use of players. The fact that these developments should attract so much attention is, to some extent, a commentary on a lack of basic understanding on the part of clubs, players, and spectators. Too often, a new system is looked upon as the solution to all problems. Players are

3

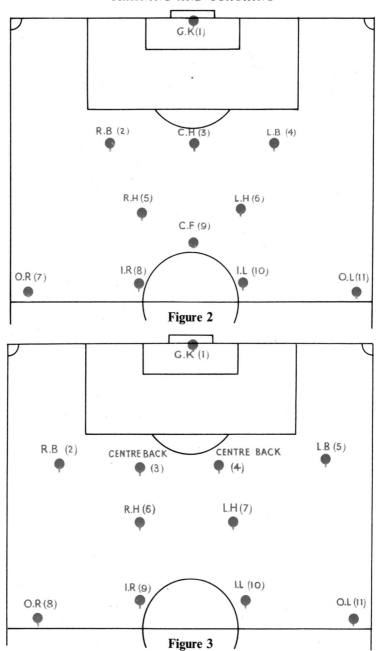

Figure 2

Figure 3

made to fit a system rather than a system being adapted to suit the players. Such a policy inevitably leads to restriction and the creative and imaginative ability of a player is submerged. Eleven basically good footballers should be able to adopt any system of play to suit the circumstances of the moment.

The basic problem for players and coaches is one of understanding. We must be capable of presenting the game in such a way as to make its problems coherent at all levels. The principles of the game must be the foundation upon which systems of play and tactical considerations are developed.

The most simple consideration is ball possession. Whenever a team loses possession of the ball, all the players in the team must, at the very least, think defensively. Obviously, some will be immediately committed defensively, either in marking opponents tightly, withdrawing in order to provide a solid last line of defence, or actually challenging an opposing player for possession. It is, nevertheless, true that all the players in the team have the main aim of regaining possession of the ball, restricting their opponents' free use of the ball while, at the same time, exposing their own goal to the minimum possible danger. Similarly when a team has possession of the ball, every member of that team should think positively about attack. It may be, for example, that the right full-back finds himself rather remote from play when his own outside-left has the ball in the far corner of the field. The right-back's adjustment may be to move much nearer to his opposing winger, thus taking himself away from a central covering position. He does so with two possibilities in mind: if play switches to his side of the field, he can move quickly in support; secondly he has tightened his marking so that if his team loses possession of the ball the opposing team will not have unrestricted scope for passing.

The first and most important principle in soccer is that ball possession determines everything. There are times when risking losing possession is justified due to an opportunity to shoot at goal. The closer it is pressing its opponents' penalty-area, the more a team is justified in taking such a risk. Conversely, the nearer a team is to its own penalty-area, the fewer should be the risks taken. Accuracy and confident control of the ball are basic requirements of players particularly when they gain possession of the ball in defensive positions.

Individually, the basic factors in a player's performance may be stated as follows:

1. Individual skill and technique
2. Understanding (intelligence)
3. Fitness (mental and physical)

5

No player can afford to miss an opportunity to improve himself in these three aspects of the game. However technically well equipped he may be, failure to study and to improve his understanding of the game will render him much less effective as a player.

Ultimately, all tactical considerations depend upon the skill and the technique of each individual player. Similarly each player's fitness will limit the degree to which he is capable of using his technique and skill in developing the team's playing strategy. Psychological fitness is also necessarily linked with the degree of physical fitness and must be acknowledged as such by a coach. These three factors are thus interdependent.

DEPTH IN ATTACK (*fig.* 4)

Generally speaking an attacking movement with depth allows the player with the ball all-round passing opportunities and, therefore, all-round support. In *fig.* 4*a* where the OR has the ball, he has a full range of passing opportunities to the positions taken up by the supporting players, IR, RH, CF, and RB.

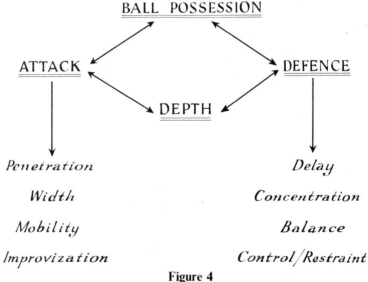

Figure 4

In *fig.* 5 where the Right Half has the ball the forward players have taken up 'flat' positions relative to each other and, presumably, will be closely marked or covered. If two of the forwards moved towards the RH (*fig.* 6) they would increase the passing possibilities open to him and at the same time present problems to the defenders who might be marking them fairly closely. The problem

6

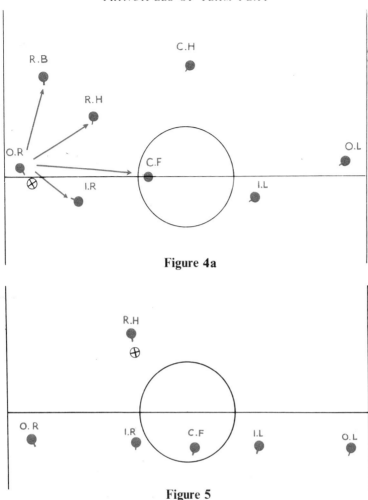

Figure 4a

Figure 5

for the defenders is whether or not to follow the attackers. If they follow their attackers they allow space to be created behind them which can be exploited by the RH's use of a through pass. If they remain in covering positions then the opposing attack is allowed a certain degree of freedom in pressing home the attacking movement. Obviously, if there is any real doubt in the minds of the defenders, they will refuse to be drawn into following the attackers.

From the coach's point of view the minimum number of players which can produce depth in attack must be three. They will find

7

themselves in some form of triangular formation, although the nature of this triangle will often change and change rapidly.

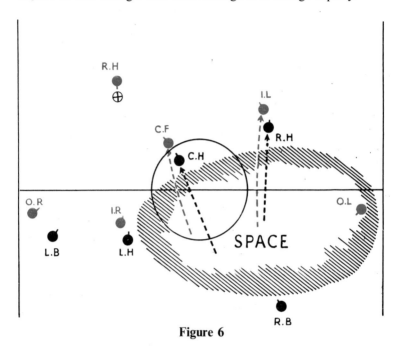

Figure 6

The formation shown in *fig.* 7 shows the OR, IR, and CF attacking in depth. This attack may develop in such a way that the IR sees an opportunity to move into an advanced position. One of the other players will balance the IR's forward run to continue to

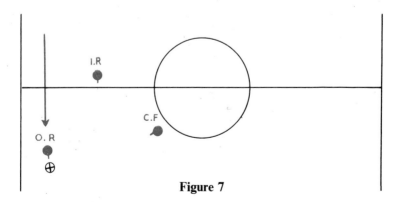

Figure 7

provide depth, as in *fig*. 8. Here the CF has tried to tempt the CH away from the centre of the field to open up a path for forward runs of the IR, and, having done this, he has folded in behind the other forwards as a supporting player. One can now see why numbers can be misleading in modern football, particularly in an attacking phase of the game. The triangle may be pointing in any

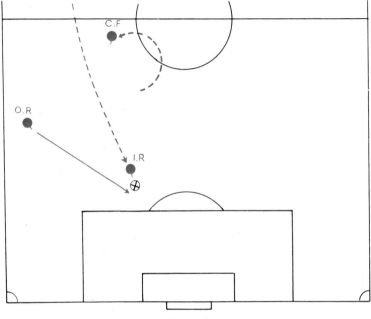

Figure 8

direction but the flatter it becomes the more the players concerned are taking risks, for the following reasons: (1) they are reducing passing possibilities; and (2) whatever passing possibilities exist in a flat attack, square passing or passing across the field must increase. When square passing increases the risk of a pass being intercepted increases.

It follows that whatever the number of players involved in attacking play they should pay attention to depth. The resultant formations may resemble squares, diamonds, 'W's or 'M's; this is unimportant. What is important is that the players should understand why depth is necessary.

9

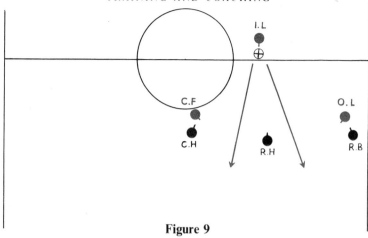

Figure 9

DEPTH IN DEFENCE

Basically the same considerations apply to depth in defence. Here we are involved in restricting space through which and into which attacking players can move with safety. The defence attempts to restrict the gaps through which passes can be made. Players cover not only each other but also the spaces for which the whole defence is responsible.

In *fig.* 9 the three defenders are lying square and thus a pass which beats one of them beats all three. Similarly they are not covering each other and, more important, they are not covering the space into which attacking players wish to move, that is, the space behind them.

In *fig.* 10 the RB and the CH have both moved away from their men in order to give cover against each other and also to threaten the space into which the IL might wish to pass the ball. He can pass to his other forwards but defenders are not beaten by the pass. Defensive structures, therefore, become a series of interlocking triangular formations and the further back they go the tighter they become.

PENETRATION IN ATTACK

The aim of a team which has possession of the ball and is, therefore, in an attacking position is to move the ball as accurately and as quickly as possible into or through the opposing defence. This is assuming that they wish to score since, at times, a team may indulge in interpassing without intending an immediate threat to the

10

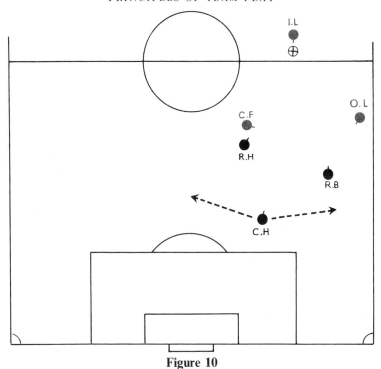

Figure 10

opposing goal. Penetrative play can develop in all the phases of the game, not only in passes which elude opposing defenders and result in a shot on goal. Indeed, the great teams are able to produce a series of penetrating passes from deep inside their own half, and the more effective their tactics the fewer these passes will be. This is not to say that a team should base its play on long passes into the opposing half of the field; the opposing side would have something to say about this. It should not be overlooked, however, that the more a team plays across the field in its preliminary passing the less effective it will be in penetration.

In *fig.* 11, where an attack has broken down, the goalkeeper has an immediate opportunity to pass the ball to his own OL who has dropped into a deep position. This is a safe pass which rarely achieves anything except ensuring that ball possession is maintained. If the circumstances are right, a pass to the feet of a central attacker (CF or IR) is much more effective. It is made deep into the opposing side and since it is to a central player it may cause a central defender to commit himself to a challenge. The pass to the winger should be the second one for which the goalkeeper looks.

11

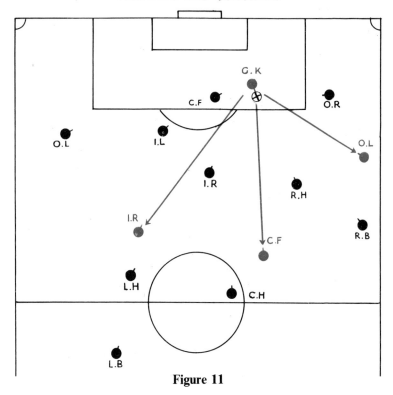

Figure 11

In this situation, it can be right if all members of the side realise and understand the attacking policy. For example, in *fig.* 12, if opposing players are blocking the path for such a pass, the goal-keeper's colleagues must clear the path for him. This particularly applies to players who normally have mid-field positions. Two situations are thus created. If opposing players do not move with them the defenders are free to receive a pass. If opposing players do move with them the channel is open for the penetration pass to the advanced forward.

Movements in which players run into positions to decoy players from certain parts of the field in order that more effective passes can be made, are known as 'decoy runs' or 'movements off the ball'. The truly intelligent player is constantly aware of the value of such movements. They are vital if a team is to become an effective attacking unit.

The creation of penetration possibilities becomes more difficult the nearer the attacking side approaches the opponents' goal since

12

the space available for control and the gaps through which passes
can be made diminish all the time.

In *fig.* 13, where the black RH is in possession of the ball, it is
obvious that the easy passes to the IL or to the OR achieve very
little since the opposing defence is still in a position to watch the
ball and attacking players in front of them. In this situation the IL
may run on the outside of the opposing RH and away from the

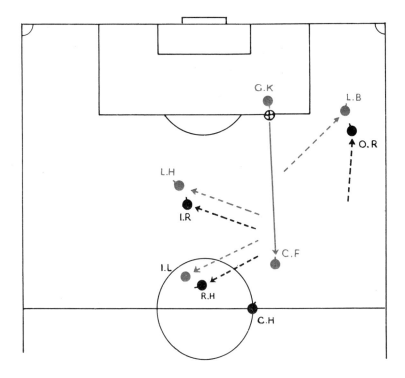

Figure 12

centre of the field. If his run is well-timed he may receive the ball
himself, but, more important, he can open up a channel for a
pass to the CF. The IR could also assist by drifting out towards
the right-wing position thus tempting the LH away from the space
in the centre of the field. Again he could be considered as a passing
possibility but he is helping to clear space for the centre-forward
which is equally important.

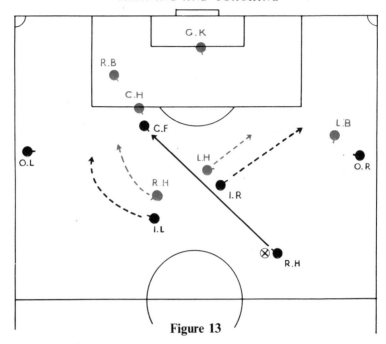

Figure 13

DELAY IN DEFENCE

Where penetration is a major objective in attack, delay must obviously be a principle of defence. This results from a clear understanding of the order of priority for a team which has lost possession of the ball.

The *first* consideration, defensively, is the goal, and this will affect play in every part of the field.

Secondly, having lost the ball, a team must be immediately aware of the space between defending players and, even more important, behind them.

Thirdly, the nearer the attacking side approaches the opposing goal the more closely they must be marked.

It will be easily appreciated from this that time is necessary for the defensive structure to be established. Instead of meeting attacking players, defenders will tend to withdraw to central defensive positions; they will tend to retreat towards their own penalty-area. Advanced players in the team (the forwards mainly) will harry players near to them and will always threaten the line of any pass intended to move the ball towards an advanced and central attacking player on the opposing side. They will try to force the side in possession of the ball to play square or across the field. Mid-field players will tighten up their marking of mid-field attackers while

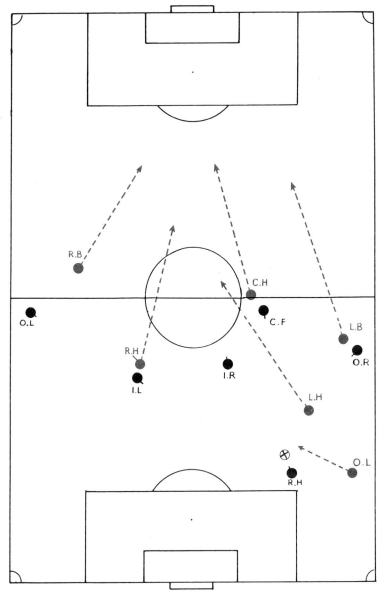

Figure 14

the rearmost defenders will adopt covering positions against possible through passes. A team which falls back in front of an opposing side almost inevitably slows it down. In this way the attack is delayed and time for defensive organization is made.

In *fig.* 14 the black RH has gained possession of the ball. The opposing OL being the nearest player at the time has moved in-field to threaten the line of possible passes to attacking forwards. All the rearmost defending players have retreated to central positions. The IR is in a dangerous position hence the need for retreat in order to gain the necessary time for another player to recover. If faced with two players who are free, a defending player, irrespective of his position on the field of play, should always mark or cover the player who is nearer to the goal which is being defended. As far as possible defenders need to see the ball and attackers who are likely to threaten at the same time.

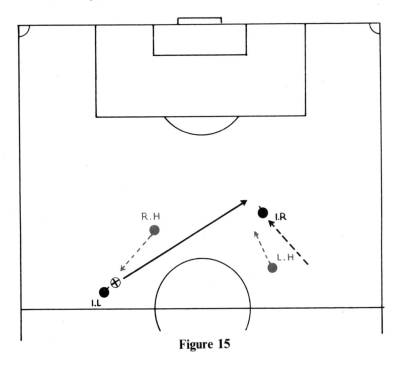

Figure 15

In *fig.* 15 the movement of the RH towards the opposing inside-left, who has the ball, opens the way for a penetration pass from the IL to the IR and the LH has not had time to retreat to a covering position. Here the RH must retreat until he can see both the IL and

16

the IR in front of him. A pass from the IL to the IR, in this situation, does not threaten immediate danger and the LH has time to recover into a position behind the RH (*fig.* 16).

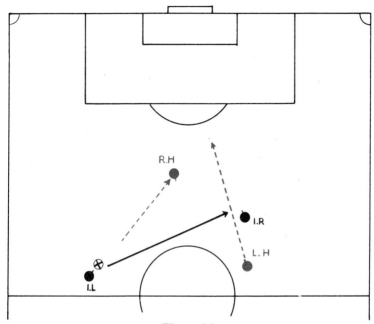

Figure 16

CONCENTRATION IN DEFENCE

From the delaying tactics and the defensive priorities which have been established, it will be obvious that the final stage of defence to be discussed is that within and around the penalty-area. Equally obviously the area which offers the greatest opportunity for scoring shots is the central part of the penalty-area. Without being too rigid, a reasonable guide to defence can be established as follows. For adult players all shots from 20-25 yards or less present a scoring threat to the defending side. It may also be said that the finer the angle of the shot, the less likely it is to score.

Two imaginary lines projecting outwards, one from each goal-post, at an angle of 45° to the goal-line, and approximately 30-35 yards in length (*fig.* 17), enclose the central zone of defence. If the foremost defenders are on the outer edge of this zone, the possibility of shots being taken from less than 30-35 yards is reduced;

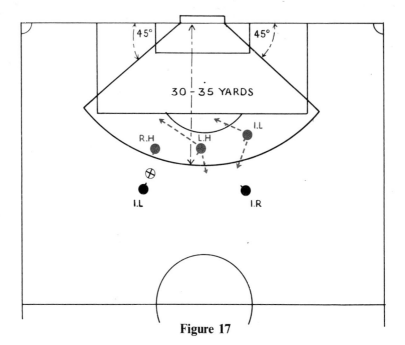

Figure 17

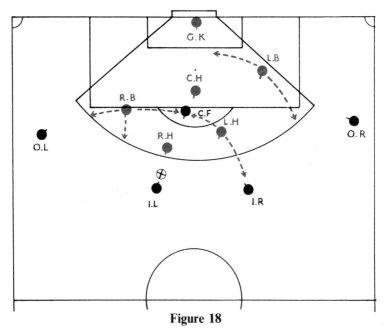

Figure 18

and if defenders are concentrated within this arc we can expect few angled shots to score since we have narrowed the angle. This is, perhaps, an over-simplification, but it will serve as a rough guide.

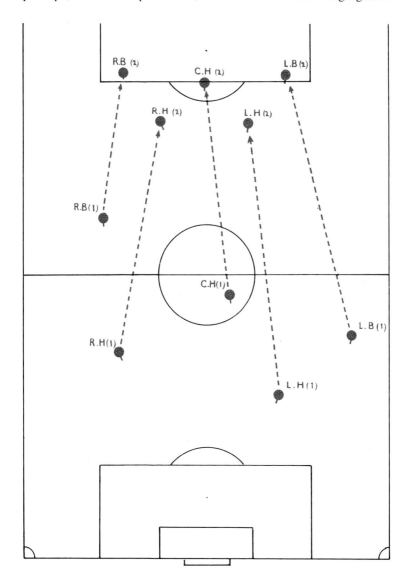

Figure 19

Just as a goalkeeper's job is governed by angles, so all defenders must take into account the angle of attack.

In *fig*. 18 the 3-2 zone defence is designed to produce maximum coverage against scoring opportunities in the most dangerous part of the field. We have already seen how necessary is delay in defensive organization and how defenders, when they are in doubt, retreat centrally and, as a result, concentrate centrally in front of goal. This retreat or withdrawal from wide positions to concentrated central defensive positions is known as 'funnelling in defence'.

In *fig*. 19 from wide positions in mid-field defenders converge into concentrated central positions in and outside the penalty-area. This concentration of players not only keeps shooting opportunities at a reasonably ineffective range but also reduces the space between defending players. This makes the exploitation of a through-pass very difficult and also allows attacking players very little time in which to control and manoeuvre the ball should such a pass reach them.

WIDTH IN ATTACK

If on the one hand defenders retreat and concentrate effectively, every attempt must be made in the attacking half of the field to

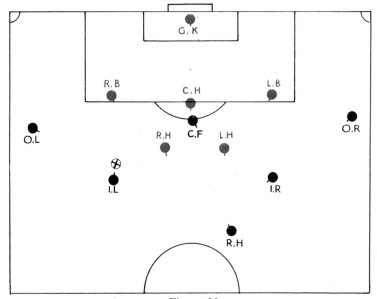

Figure 20

tempt the defenders away from concentrated defensive positions. This can only be achieved if the attacking side has passing opportunities over the whole width of the field.

In *fig.* 20 the defending side is retreating and concentrating. If the attacking players, particularly on the wings, follow them into the space outside the penalty-area they will make this space even more restricted than it is. By having players in wide positions the attack may tempt defending players away from central positions. This particularly applies where one or more defenders have a liking for the physical challenge. Players of this type take risks in order to be in a position to tackle for the ball; they therefore take up positions slightly nearer to whichever of the attacking players are in their particular sector of the defence.

It is an inescapable fact that however well-organized a defence may be, and however restrained the individual players within it, human nature still plays its part. Any group of players who are subjected to the physical and psychological pressure of attack for long periods will tend to become anxious. A defending side is only relaxed if it succeeds in regaining possession of the ball within a reasonable space of time, and the longer this time lasts the less

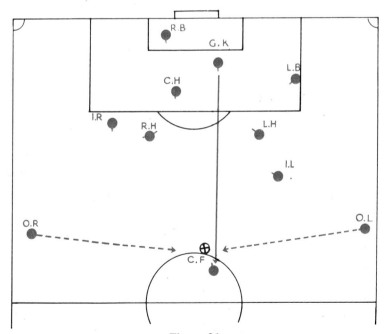

Figure 21

relaxed and confident they become. The less confident they become the greater the risks which they may be tempted to take. Psychological pressure is thus a factor which must be allowed for in all tactical considerations.

In a system of play which may be heavily defensive, width in attack may seem to be not so necessary. There is little point in having two players wide on the touch lines when a team plays with three forwards for the greater part of the game. When the ball is released from defence it is, initially, far more important that the receiving player shall obtain immediate support. In this situation both wingers may move quickly to support the centre-forward, or one winger and the centre-forward may move across field to support the second winger as in *fig.* 21 *and* 22. Here the immediate

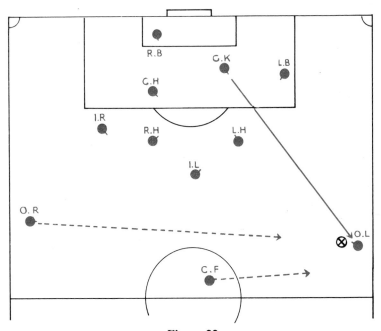

Figure 22

concern is to provide whatever support in depth is possible for the benefit of the player receiving the ball. Since a three-man attack is at a heavy numerical disadvantage they will try to minimize the disadvantage by all moving to a more restricted part of the field. By doing this they may also cause the opposing defence to move over, thus creating an opportunity for width to be re-established by players who break out from defence quickly on the flanks, *fig.* 23. In other words by loading their attack on one side of the field they create the possibility of a break-through on that side, but

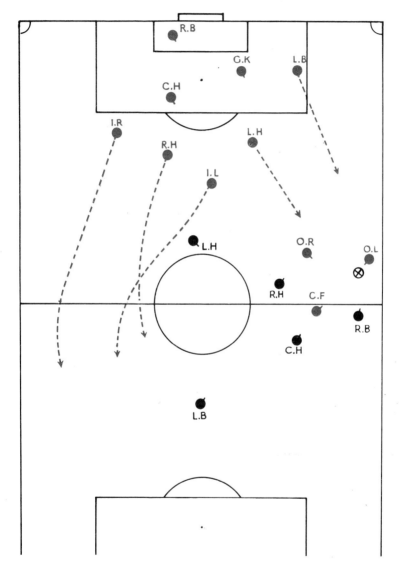

Figure 23

they also create a chance for players to adopt effective wide positions on the far side of the field.

This generalization on width in attack is much more applicable
to the preparation or building-up phase of attacking play. When a
team is attempting to strike at goal, chances have to be taken and
decisions made quickly. In this phase of the game, however, width
should be maintained and, if lost, re-established as quickly as
possible.

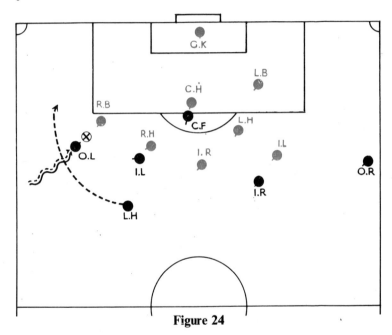

Figure 24

In *fig.* 24 the attacking side is faced with a concentrated and
balanced defence. The OL has moved in-field to attack the right
flank of the defence and he has thus narrowed the attacking front.
The attack is well supported and the LH has run outside his own
OL. He has thus created an overlap and threatens to turn the flank
of the defence. At this stage the OL can continue to attack along
his original line but the defence and particularly covering defenders
must be aware of the threat which is created by the LH's wide run.

MOBILITY IN ATTACK

From the examples used to illustrate the necessity for delay and
concentration in defence, it is apparent that defensive play lends

itself to easy organization. A defending team is waiting for mistakes; it may, at the same time, actively encourage the opposing
side to make them. Provided that there is a clear understanding of
priorities the defensive organization of a team can be simple and
yet extremely effective in its simplicity. This can be easily proved by
allowing eight or nine players to attack a goal which is defended by
four or five players. The number of scoring shots will be very few,
indeed the number of shooting attempts may even be low. This is
because the attack is within reach of goal which demands precision
and care. The defence is concerned with merely stopping the
attack and, therefore, their work demands less accuracy; they can
merely kick the ball out of play, a tactic crude but remarkably
effective.

In attacking play, too much organization can be restrictive. As
players are faced with the problems created by a defence, they must
be allowed to experiment with solutions. They will have a basic
attacking plan and they may well have 'set' or rehearsed plays,
but they must be encouraged to react naturally and intelligently to
new problems.

One of the means employed to disturb a defence is to continually
change the positions of the attacking players. A defender who is

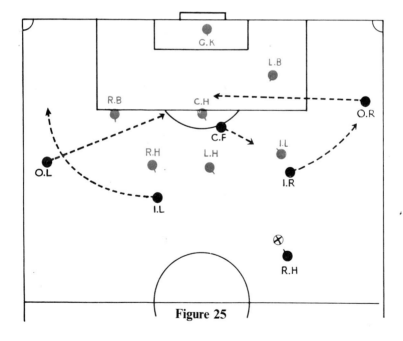

Figure 25

dealing with the same opponent in the same part of the field for the whole game has a relatively easy task, and he learns far more about the attacker's play than the attacker learns about his. This is a natural consequence of the negative side of defensive play. Defenders faced with different opponents interchanging their positions intelligently are often puzzled.

This is best illustrated by the use of diagonal running and overlap running by an attacking side which is trying to deal with a well organized and concentrated defence on the edge of that defence's penalty-area. Here are some of the interchanges which might be effective in *fig*. 25 where the RH has the ball: the OR moves across field to the CF position; the CF has moved towards the IR position to offer himself as a target for RH's pass; it is likely that the CH will have followed him and thus the interchange between himself and the OR could leave the OR as the new centre-forward and relatively free from a defender. Similarly the IR could assist by running outside the OR; he has then cleared space for the centre-forward should the RH wish to pass to him. The OL may have decided to try a diagonal run behind the CH either for a pass or to create a diversion by drawing attention to himself. The IL could then run outside the full-back, perhaps taking an opposing central

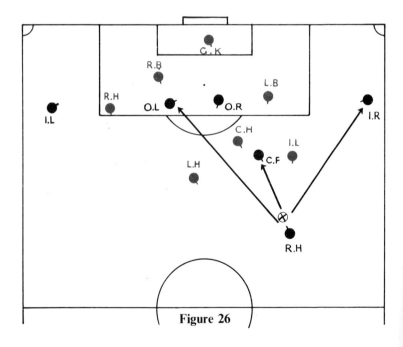

Figure 26

defender with him and also re-establishing wide passing possibilities in attack. We now have an attack with players in the positions shown in *fig.* 26.

The employment of diagonal movements achieves two purposes. The first, as we have seen, is to shake the confidence of defenders by surprising them. The second is concerned with space; all the movements of attacking players near the penalty-area have to be watched closely and judged quickly by defenders. They are never quite certain whether a player is moving to receive a pass or to tempt a defender away from a position in which some other attacker may receive it.

The most refined use of the skill of diagonal running occurs when the player can run into positions in which he is an immediate danger himself, should he receive the ball, and in which, at the same time, he has opened up the possibility of a pass to someone who is just as dangerously placed. A further generalization on diagonal running is that the nearer the attack comes to its opponents' final defensive positions, the flatter the angle of the run must be.

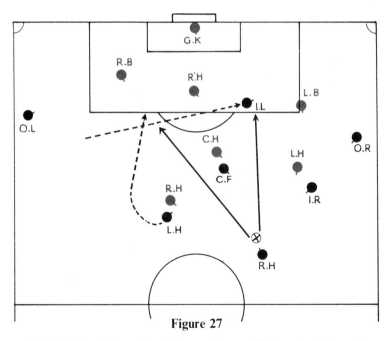

Figure 27

In *fig.* 27 the IL has timed his run diagonally into the IR position to coincide with the turn and run of the LH. For the opposing RH, choice of action is difficult. Should he follow the IL and block the threat to the goal, or should he cover the threat which is posed by the run of the LH.

It will also be seen that the more direct is the run towards goal the more positive must be the reaction of a defender. A straight run towards goal by an attacker must be covered. In other words, the problem of a choice of action is solved for the defender. Naturally such a run, if it is successful, usually results in a goal-scoring chance. The conclusion to be drawn is that the more all the forwards adopt this kind of attacking run, the more easily the attack will be stopped.

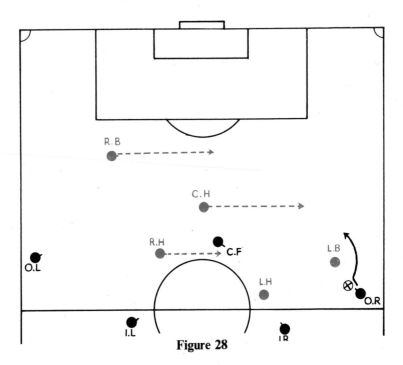

Figure 28

BALANCE IN DEFENCE

From the analysis of the need for mobility in attack it is apparent that defensive play is concerned with the maintenance of cover at all times. If the movement of attacking players is calculated to draw defenders out of position in order to free other attackers, and also to create attacking space, then the defence must be balanced against these threats. Attacking play aims at getting through,

28

around, or over defensive players and thus any lack of balance in defensive organization will allow these aims to be achieved.

Let us take the diagonal system of covering which used the two full-backs and the centre-half as its key units.

In *fig.* 28 where play is developing on the LB's side of the field, cover can be afforded by both CH and RB if the LB is beaten. If the CF moves out to the wing behind the LB he is threatening to unbalance the defence. If the defensive organization is good then the LB may leave his opposing winger and mark the player who has taken up the new wing position (the CF) in *fig.* 29.

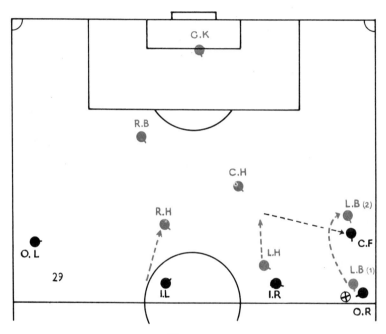

Figure 29

This means that the cover is still intact and the defence is still balanced against a breakthrough on the left side of the field. If the CH follows the CF out to the wing, however, cover remains but balance is destroyed immediately (*fig.* 30).

A large space has been created in mid-field which can become an immediate passage to goal. The RB can move across to check this threat but now the same amount of space has been left on his defensive flank. We can also see how the same situation may affect

the positions of the wing-half backs in this defensive structure.
In *fig*. 31 the RH has dropped back to fill the gap left by the CH

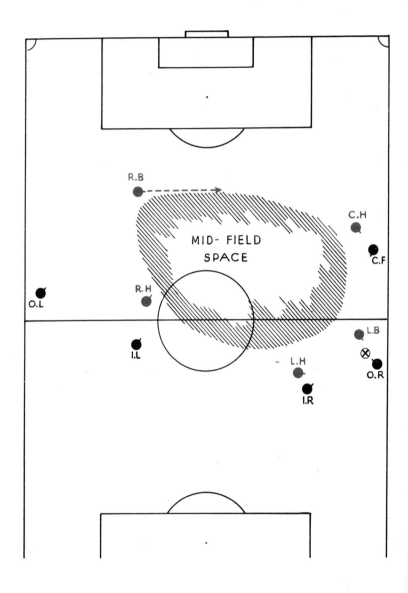

Figure 30

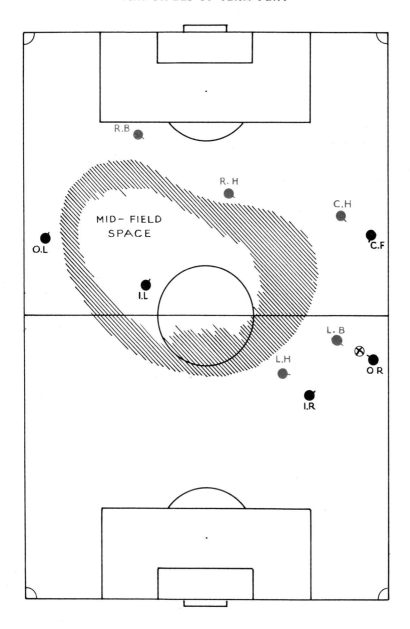

Figure 31

and has thus re-established balance at the rear of the defence. At the same time, however, his new role has left a large space in the inside-left position which may be exploited if play can be switched from right to left quickly enough. If this exploitation is quick and accurate, it will cause one or the other of the defenders on that side of the field to be drawn out of position. It is now obvious how delay will be necessary in order that balance can be re-established.

It is not uncommon for attackers to be tightly marked by defenders, particularly when a side's tactical plan is based upon stopping one outstanding attacking player. Where such a player finds himself subjected to tight marking throughout the game he knows that his access to the ball will be severely limited. Thus, he will try to take the opposing defender into positions where his absence from the final defensive positions may cause the maximum

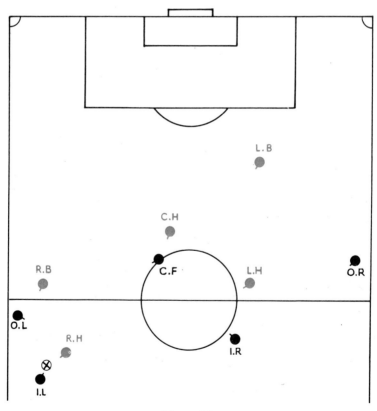

Figure 32

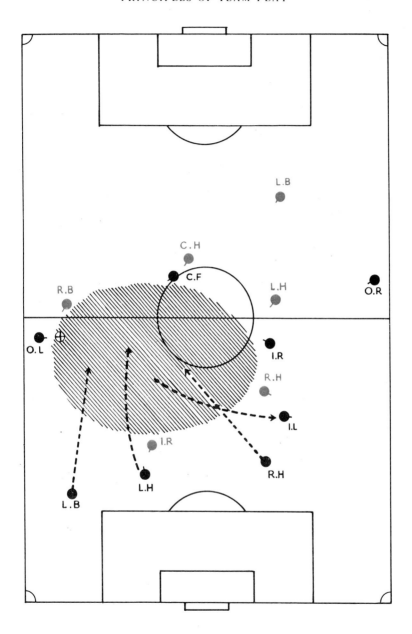

Figure 33

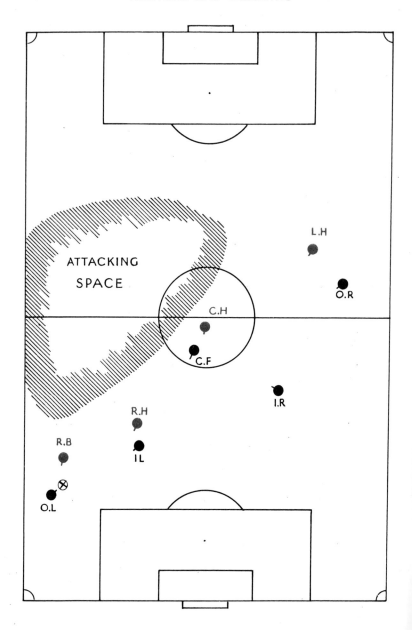

Figure 34

amount of trouble. Let us imagine an inside-forward who is receiving close attention from an opposing wing-half. If he merely moves into other forward positions he will be followed by the wing-half and the rest of the defenders will cover accordingly.

In *fig.* 32 the IL has moved into a wing position and the defensive balance remains intact.

In *fig.* 33 the IL has moved wide and deep into his own half and virtually joined his own right-half. If the space thus created between the opposing RH and the other defenders can be exploited these defenders can be drawn. This may be achieved by a temporary change of positions whereby the IL now becomes the right-half and the right-half moves into an attacking rôle. The use of a deep lying centre-forward in setting problems for the rigid stopper centre-half achieved the same effect. These problems will always be created for defenders who are used in tight, man-for-man marking duties. In the same way the use of one wing-man as the principle link player between attack and defence is aimed at destroying the balance of a defence.

In *fig.* 34 if the RB moves to mark the OL he leaves a great deal of space unguarded behind him. If the right-half is detailed to mark the OL, space is again left within the defensive structure. One method used to counter the use of a deep lying wing-man involved a return to the sytem of play which was widespread before the introduction of the present offside-law. Wing-halves marked wingers and full-backs marked inside forwards.

In conclusion, therefore, we may say that the more rigid the man-for-man marking duties of defenders become, the more likely it is that the defence will become unbalanced. Marking space is much more important than marking players. The nearer one moves towards one's own goal the more the two objectives become the same thing. In and outside its own penalty-area a team aims at restricting space and also the free movement of attackers. It is still true, however, that even in this situation space can provide a bigger problem than attackers.

CONTROL AND RESTRAINT IN DEFENCE

Consideration of depth, delay, and balance in defence means an emphasis on restraint in this aspect of the game. Defensive play necessitates a high awareness of risk and the priorities which must be recognized when the opposing side has possession of the ball. Players who are defensively employed, and this means the whole of a team when possession has been lost, must pay close attention to their function relative to all the other players in the team. For example, if a winger loses possession of the ball to an opposing

35

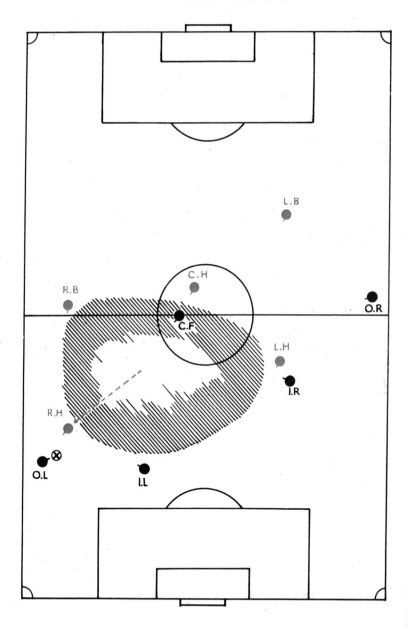

Figure 35

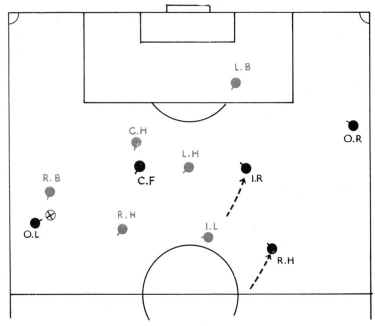

Figure 36

full-back, perhaps in a position close to the full-back's own goal-line, a wild challenge which enables the full-back to beat him is bad defensive play on the winger's part. The challenge may have been spectacular but the mere fact that the full-back beats the winger is enough to expose other members of the defending side.

The higher the level of football the more likely it is that the side with the ball will be able to take advantage of such weaknesses. There are certain examples of lack of restraint in defensive play which typify the problems involved. The first is the player who is always drawn towards the ball.

This might be the RH in *fig.* 35 who, finding himself nearer to the OL than his own RB, is drawn out to make a challenge. In being drawn he exposes a gap between himself, the CH and the LH. The RB dare not move forward to fill the space since by doing so he will leave space behind both himself and the RH. If he moves forward he and the right-half will be square for a short time and therefore open to penetration. Control is shown by the RH when he falls back into a normal defensive position where he can watch developments as they occur, in front of him. The winger with the ball is not an immediate threat since all defensive players are

37

balanced in covering rôles. In exactly the same way the centre-forward who rushes towards the goalkeeper chasing a through-pass which he has no hope of catching, shows no restraint. Having drawn the CF the goalkeeper can immediately set up play to one of his defenders who will in turn cause another opposing player to be drawn.

A second factor influencing the stability of a defence is the extent to which players watch the ball. In defence the restriction of space is of major importance and particularly, as we have seen, space between and behind defensive players. The danger in watching the ball, especially when it is not within playing range, is that attackers can move onto the 'blindside' of defenders and into spaces behind them. A natural consequence of ball watching is that the player forgets his defensive responsibilities and tends to react to the movement of the ball.

In *fig.* 36 where the ball is held by the OL, the IR has moved onto the blind side of the defending LH. This is the side of the player furthest away from the ball. In the event of play being switched by a cross-field pass, the defending LB is caught between two players. In the same way the attacking RH is threatening to move onto the blind side of the defending IL. Attackers can only achieve this when the defenders' attention is drawn towards the ball. It follows that defenders should always be aware of those attackers who are trying to move behind them.

Football is, in many respects, a test of patience. Defenders restrain themselves in order that when they challenge, they either stand a very good chance of getting the ball themselves or other defenders stand a good chance of getting it. In attack, a team tests the patience of the defending side by tempting defenders to make a badly calculated challenge. It is fairly true to say that the nearer play moves towards the penalty-area the greater the degree of control and restraint which must be exercised by defending players.

IMPROVISATION IN ATTACK

Since modern defensive play is highly. organized, methods of attack must be unlimited. The tactical use of a team's strengths in attack is, of course, important but their rigid application is erroneous. When an attacking player with the ball is faced by an opponent, the decision as to how to beat him is entirely with the attacker. He will have tried to assess the various strengths and weaknesses of the opposing defenders, and although a great deal of information may be available about individual opposing players before a match commences, it will be only a fragment of the knowledge required to ensure that they are beaten regularly. If it were possible to acquire fullest knowledge of players in the opposing team, the problem of coaching a team to combine effectively against them would be greatly simplified.

For example, a team may have decided that its attacking strength is in the ability of its wingers to beat opposing full-backs on the outside. The basic attacking plan might be to isolate opposing full-backs, leaving the winger to attack the full-back alone. Crossfield passes might also be used from the inside-forward and the wing-halves to try to use the winger's speed. This is fine, as an attacking formation, but in a game one of the wingers may find that he is more easily able to beat the full-back on the inside. If this is so the attack must be adaptable enough to exploit this alternative.

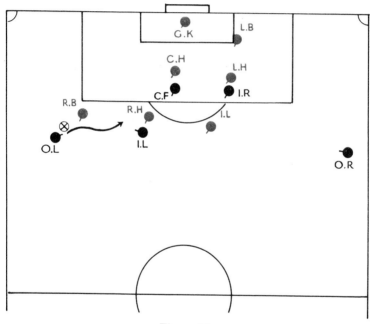

Figure 37

In *fig*. 37 if the OL moves inside his full-back he will merely move into an area already congested by players. The aim of his other forwards will be to clear the area for him and create better opportunities to exploit the full-back's weakness.

In *fig*. 38 the attacking IL has run diagonally across the RB

thus attempting to draw the RH into a covering position behind
the RB. Both the attacking CF and his IR have attempted to move
behind their opponents thus trying to draw them away from the
centre of the field. The OR has moved away from the opposing
LB in order to retain depth. This full-back is now concerned with
his covering responsibilities towards the centre of the field and he
also has to be aware of the possibility of the ball being played to
the OR.

To overcome organized defensive play, a great deal of movement
is required from opposing attackers to commit the defenders to
false positions. Some of the movement will be to receive passes but
a great deal of it will be aimed at creating opportunities for other
attackers.

One of the most important skills which any player can possess
is the ability to take on and beat an opponent with the ball. This
skill is just as important to a full-back as it is to a winger, yet it is
far too often ignored in the coaching of players at all levels. Whenever and wherever an opponent is beaten the player who has been
successful has created difficulties for the opposing defence. He has

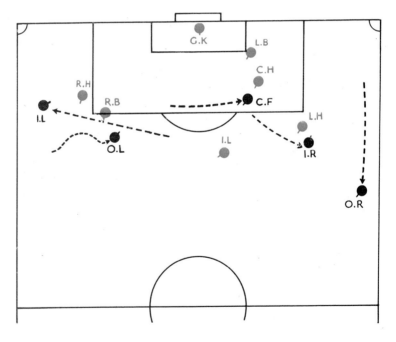

Figure 38

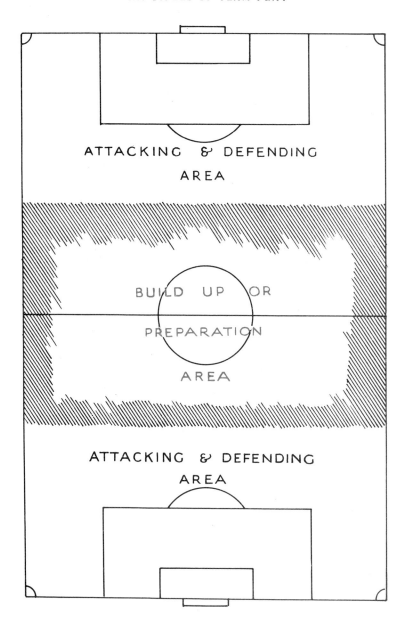

Figure 39

established a position where the attacking side has a spare man—
himself! The use of situations in the game where an attacking side
has one or more players spare is a most important aspect of attacking football and one to which a great deal of attention must be
given in coaching and training. In the final attacking phase of the
game, that is to say just outside and inside the opponents' penalty-
area, the ability of an attacker to dribble and beat an opposing
defender is of great value. This is a part of the field where defenders
must tackle with care since a careless tackle can result in the award
of a penalty-kick. It follows, therefore, that players who are gifted
in their ability to dribble around an opponent should reserve this
ability in the main for that part of the field where it is likely to be
most effective. To show all one's tricks in mid-field is to give
opposing players too much information and in this less dangerous
area the defenders will learn far more than the attackers.

Generally speaking the field can be divided into three areas
(fig. 39). The attacking area is the one in which, for example,
wingers capable of taking on a full-back will be most effective.
It is occasionally true that quick, attacking breaks from deep
defensive positions are successful. This particularly applies where
a team supports its attack heavily and where its defenders are
drawn into square positions. Here they leave the maximum amount
of space behind them into which the ball can be played and into
which opposing forwards can move. Today, however, when teams
are much more aware of space and tend to restrict it very quickly
when opponents have the ball, this attacking move has to be used
sparingly. This assumes, of course, that the so-called long-passing
game or the short-passing game represent two extremes. A good
team will use both according to the play of their opponents. To use
a succession of short passes emphasizes accuracy but lacks speed.
Where there is the possibility for a long, accurate pass in achieving
penetration this should be used. Obviously to build the whole of an
attacking system upon the long pass is emphasizing speed and
directness at the expense of control and accuracy. There can be no
simple solution to attacking problems, but players must be encouraged to consider the variety of ways by which a defence or a
defender may be exposed.

2 Systems
of Play

A system of play is a recognizable pattern of play resulting from the use of certain players in fairly clearly defined functions on the field. Systems of play must be sufficiently elastic to enable the different individual strengths of players to be used to the maximum effect and, also, to allow temporary changes to take place according to the problems which may be posed by different opposing teams.

Having adopted a certain system of play, a team may find that the opposing team is using a different system of play which sets a problem. Possibly the opposing centre-forward may move into deep positions and link up with his own half-back, perhaps leaving the two inside-forwards to work as twin centre-forwards. If the three back system in defence is employed against such an attack, this will leave the centre-half with two men to deal with, a situation which results in marked defensive weaknesses. Obviously the three back system of play must be changed slightly to meet the new attacking threat.

There are two extreme schools of thought which are represented by the following points of view. The first is that the game should be played on a man-to-man basis, that is, in all phases of the game, each player in a team must be responsible for dealing with his opposite number. The goalkeepers are thought to cancel themselves out since they are only remotely concerned with free play over the field as a whole. The second school of thought maintains that football is a game based upon space and, provided that a team can command space effectively, the problems of opposing players need not be too difficult to deal with.

43

There are arguments for and against both schools. In a rigid man-for-man system of play, it is unrealistic to expect each man in a team to mark his opposite number for ninety minutes. If an opponent breaks free with the ball, the system is destroyed if he is quick enough to exploit whatever advantage he has gained. He should be able to run through the opposing defence unopposed. What really happens, of course, is that the defending team withdraws, hoping to gain time in order that the man-for-man balance can be re-established by the quick recovery of any player who has been beaten. If this does not happen then the defenders slide over to counter the immediate threat thus leaving an attacker free in the least dangerous part of the field.

It should be made clear at this stage that there are not two halves of a team in football named defence and attack. A side defends or attacks depending on whether or not it has possession of the ball. The responsibility for defending or attacking belongs to each player in a team as the situation in play demands it.

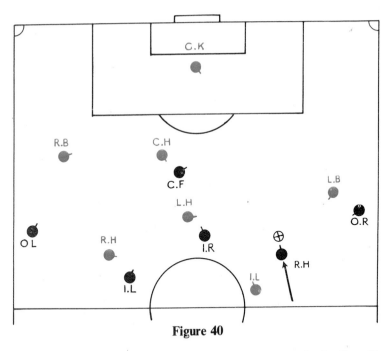

Figure 40

In *fig.* 40 where the RH has broken clear of a defender he will obviously make a direct approach on goal. Depending on how quickly the IL recovers to challenge him, the RH will either draw another defender or pass the ball through the defence. The defensive counter might be to slide across from right to left.

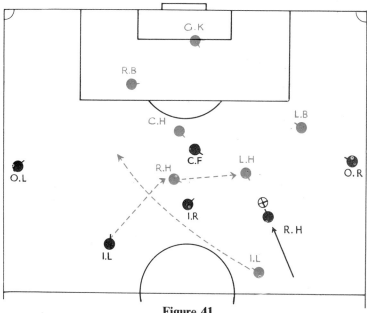

Figure 41

In *fig.* 41 the LH has moved across to block the opposing player's threat to goal. His RH has moved across to mark the opposing IR and the RB has moved towards his own goal and away from the opposing IL and OL. It can be seen, therefore, that rigid man-for-man play in this situation is impossible. It should be said here that a man is being marked tightly when an opponent is within immediate challenging distance. The higher the class of football, the shorter this distance will be since good players can take advantage of the smallest amount of freedom. As we shall see later, there are times in a game when tight man-for-man marking has considerable advantages. But it should be noted (*fig.* 40) that tight man-for-man marking means rejection of the basic principles of defence since the defending players' positions are determined entirely by their opponents.

Exponents of the 'space' system in team play, would not be concerned with restraining individual opponents by marking them. They would contend that if the important spaces are filled, opposing

45

players, sooner or later, must come into these spaces. They would advocate full and immediate retreat as soon as the opposing team gained possession of the ball. This retreat would continue in front of the attack until it reached the defenders' penalty-area.

Basically there is much to be said for this system in principle but it ignores two important factors. The first is that a team should aim at containing play in the opposing half of the field for as long as possible. Secondly, a player who is in possession of the ball, and the players who are within effective passing range, should not be allowed complete freedom in which to build up attacking movements. As with the other extreme point of view, gifted individual players will make nonsense of any attempt to beat them by using rigid systems of play.

'W-M' FORMATION

This is the pattern of play which was developed following the change in the offside law in 1925. This allowed much more scope for attacking players to take up advanced positions. In consequence teams began to pay much more attention to defensive organization and particularly to the covering responsibilities of defenders. To cope with the central threat, the centre-half was withdrawn to become a third or centre-back and the two wing half-backs were positioned much more centrally to control the defensive half of the mid-field area (*fig.* 42).

In *fig.* 42 we see the resultant 'M' formation. Domination of the mid-field area assumed great importance since it was from this area that most attacking moves were begun. This caused most teams to withdraw both inside-forwards to produce a unit of four players (the inside-forwards and the wing half-backs) in the rough form of a mid-field square. Since this left the wingers and the centre-forward as the major striking units the 'W' formation in attack can clearly be seen as the basic pattern of play (*fig.* 43).

Arsenal F.C. is often credited with having introduced this system to English football. The system, which was developed by Herbert Chapman, recognized all the basic principles of play and, at the same time, brilliantly analyzed the difficulties which most teams experienced in adapting their play to the new offside law. Centre-halves who had been mid-field attacking players before 1925 were being asked to adopt purely defensive roles and to accept the responsibility for the cover given to both full-backs. Wingers were now free from the marking attention of the wing half-backs and, therefore, space could be found out on the wings, and often behind full-backs, for the quick exploitation of attacks. At the same time,

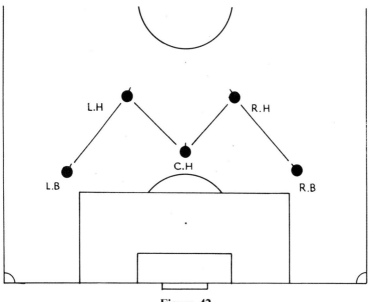

Figure 42

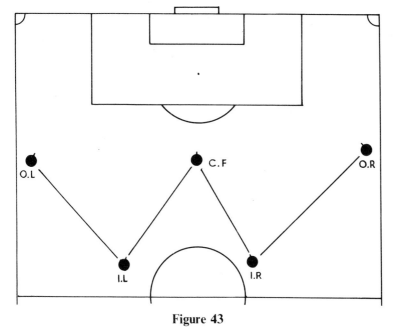

Figure 43

Chapman realized that certain areas of the field are much more important, defensively speaking, than others. The basis of his defensive system was that the area in front of goal must be the most important area on the field. Secondly, he realized that it is when a team is heavily committed to attack, and particularly when

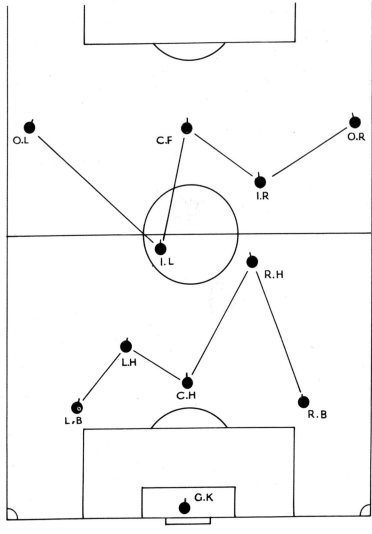

Figure 44

there is no evidence of cover between the three backs, that the attacking team is most vulnerable to a counter attack. Obviously a team which is heavily committed in attack must leave space behind it into which long passes can be played. Out of this reasoning came the following playing requirements:

1. The diagonal defence which hinged around the stopper centre-half.
2. The organization of a strong defence from which quick attacks could be launched.
3. The use of one or two players to control the build up of attacking movements.
4. The need for fast, powerful, and direct striking forwards: the two wingers and the centre-forward.

The left-half became a major defensive unit with the right-half rather less rigidly restricted and able to support the inside-left. This player (the IL) was required to initiate most of the attacking moves, principally by the use of long passes to the wingers or past

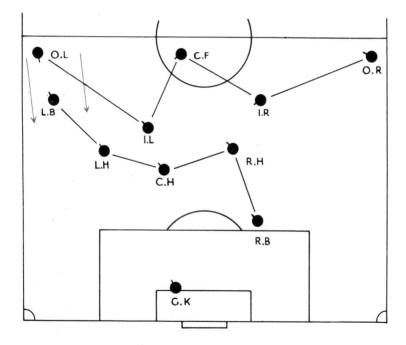

Figure 45

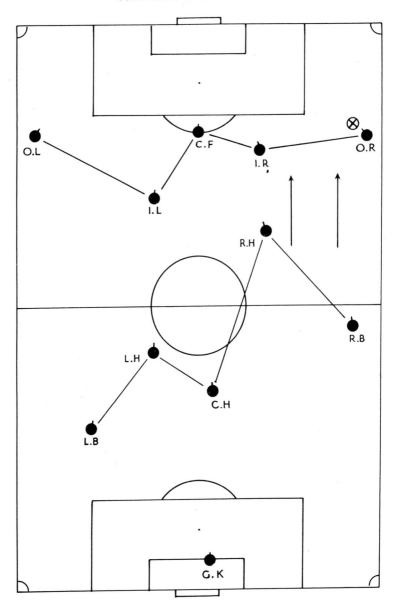

Figure 46

opposing defenders. The wingers, together with the centre-forward, were the advanced attacking units. They were supported by the inside-right who had a less restricted role in attack (*fig.* 44). It is interesting to note the similarity between this adaptation of 'W-M' play and the modern 4-2-4 system. The basic difference being in the stopper centre-half position in 'M' defence and the double centre-half play in 4-2-4.

Defensively placed and covering against an attack down its left flank the 'W-M' system of the Arsenal would have appeared as in *fig.* 45.

In an attack down the right flank, the system would have taken shape the other way round (*fig.* 46).

Because of the well-defined duties of the left-half (in defence) and the inside-left (as the main supplier of attacking passes) the shapes of the 'W' and the 'M' become lop-sided.

The 'W-M' system was developed to suit a changed situation in football, in this case a change brought about by an alteration in the Laws of the Game. Widespread imitation followed in the worst possible way. Instead of attempting to solve the problems of 'W-M' through the application and development of skill, clubs tried to use physical means to counter it. The three-man striking units were required to be direct players and, therefore, the three backs became essentially physical players where strength and size counted for a great deal. Where it was difficult to find a highly skilful passer of the ball, then both inside-forwards were withdrawn into the mid-field position. In other words, the defensive and, subsequently, the negative aspect of play was emphasized. Size, power, and speed assumed great importance in countering skill. Players were given strictly defined functions with the result that the use of truly creative and imaginative play decreased. As we have seen in discussing the principles of play, attacking play must suffer under these circumstances because a team not only becomes restricted in its play, but also restricted in its thinking.

DEEP CENTRE-FORWARD

The rigidity of the 'W-M system', particularly when it was based on man-for-man marking, was clearly exposed when further consideration was given to the requirements of space in playing the game (*fig.* 47). Where the 'W' attacking formation is used an 'M' defence is designed to give depth and, at the same time, to allow defenders to mark their opposite numbers in attack. If the CF is withdrawn to a mid-field position and if the two inside-forwards are moved forward to positions where they operate as twin centre-

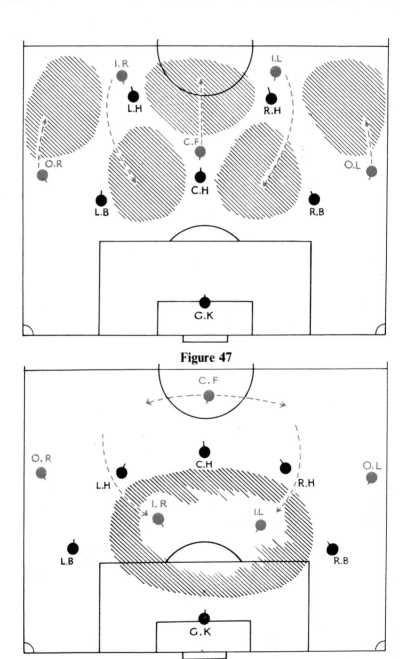

Figure 47

Figure 48

forwards, a problem is set for the defence. The two inside-forwards will attempt to draw the centre-half into false positions across the field. If the inter-change of positions is timed well so that the CF moves away from the centre-half towards the ball at the same time as one or both of the inside-forwards move into central attacking positions, marking problems become very difficult (*fig.* 48).

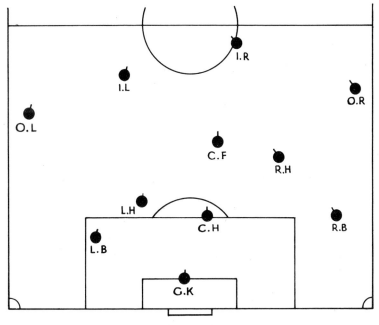

Figure 49

If the CH is drawn forward into a position between or in front of his wing half-back, space has been left into which the two inside-forwards can move. Where this interchange is performed quickly, this is a most effective system. Where, for example, the three inside-forwards, together with one wing half-back, are interchangeable in attack and defence, the problem for a defence becomes great indeed. This again emphasizes the importance of interchange of position and function in attacking football. Rigidly imposed the 'deep centre-forward' plan is no more of a problem than any other system of play (*fig.* 49).

Although their method of play placed rather more emphasis on the controlled build-up of attacking movements, the Hungarian side in the 1950s used much the same basic pattern of play as did the

Arsenal under Chapman. Controlled build-up of play (*fig.* 50) requires a greater use of the short-passing game, but it would be wrong to consider short passes more effective than long passes. In certain phases of the game each have their place. The fundamental difference between the two systems was that the Hungarians used interchange of position to a much greater extent than the Arsenal. Secondly, they relied upon skill and speed in attack whereas the Arsenal emphasis was essentially upon direct methods using power and speed.

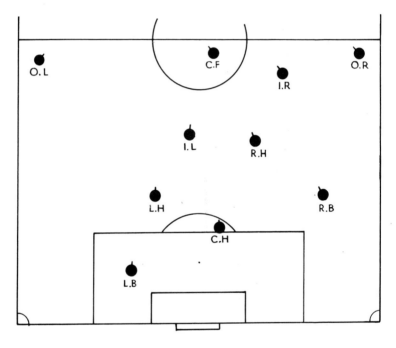

Figure 50

The diagonal cover of the 'third back' system of play has certain advantages and disadvantages when related to a 'W' attacking system where there is one central attacking unit, the centre-forward. In *fig.* 51 any movement of the centre-forward away from the centre of the field can be covered to a great extent by the centre-half. He, in turn, is covered diagonally by the full-back who is not immediately concerned with the attacking movement. In *fig.* 51 this is the right-back.

Where a team plays twin centre-forwards the problem is rather

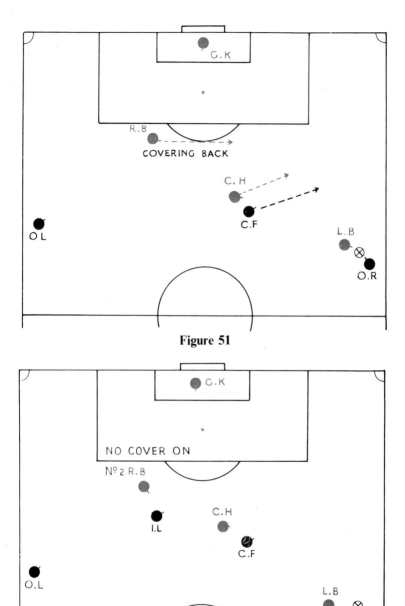

Figure 51

Figure 52

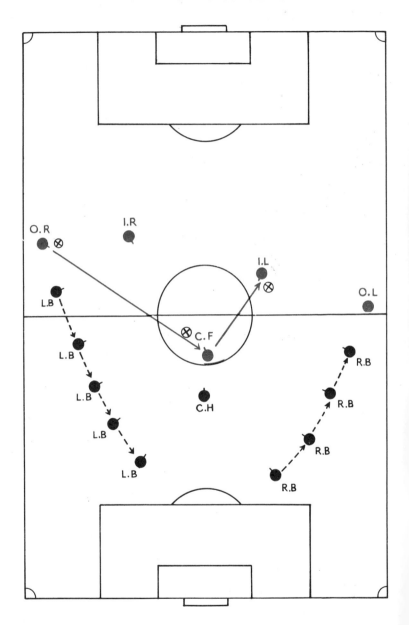

Figure 53

different since the second centre-forward can play up on the covering full-back and there is no further cover. In other words the full-back can no longer pivot freely to cover the centre of the field and the opposing wing man on his own side of the field (*fig.* 52). The pivoting movement itself is rather laborious since quick changes in the direction of an attack across the field cause the three rearmost defenders to be square or almost square for too long. In *fig.* 53, where play is built up by the red outside-right, as the ball is moved across the field to CF and then to IL, the left-back begins to swing back behind the centre-half. Similarly, the right-back begins to swing out and onto the opposing outside-left. As the two full-backs pivot so the centre-half is left in a position where there is no cover since he and the two backs are in line, square across the field.

To counter twin centre-forward play, it is obviously necessary to withdraw one of the wing half-backs in order to achieve free cover in defence.

In *fig.* 54 attack is developing on the defensive left flank. The LB is closely engaged and so is the LH, who is marking one of the two

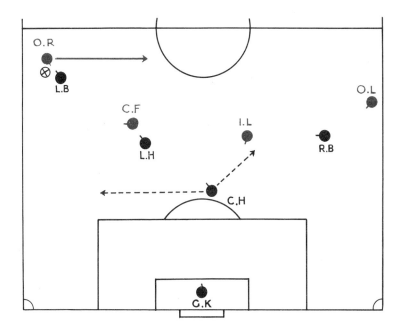

Figure 54

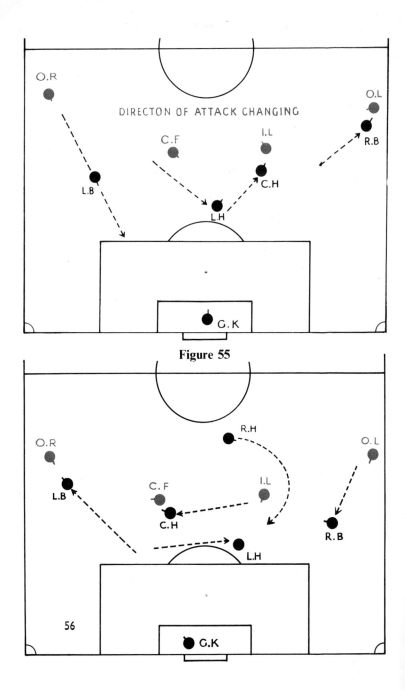

Figure 55

DIRECTON OF ATTACK CHANGING

56

centre-forwards. Cover is provided by the CH, who guards again
the possibility of an attacking break-through behind his LH ar
LB. If play is switched across the field he can move into a markin
position upon the IL while the LH will move away from the CF
and behind the centre-half (*fig.* 55).

The distances covered in this pivot are obviously greatly reduced
although the square position is still dangerous as the two central
defenders change their duties. This form of central cover allows
the full-backs to mark both wingers much more closely than was
possible in the 'three-back' system of diagonal cover.

A further development has involved the use of one covering
defender all the time. In *fig.* 56 play has switched once again
towards the attacking right flank.

Using the sliding system of marking, the centre-half has moved
across, following the change in the direction of the attack, to mark
the opposing CF. The defending left-half has merely adjusted his
position slightly in order that he remains the rearmost covering
defender. Using a central defender to cover all other defenders by
moving across the field is known as using 'a sweeper'. This defender
is responsible for covering all defensive gaps.

This is much more acceptable defensively since the duties of the
players are simplified and the centre of the field has cover all the
time. It will also be noticed that as play moves away from one side
of the field the full-back who has been marking fairly tightly moves
away from his winger to a more central position where he can watch
the movements of the winger and the nearest inside forward. He
has not, however, moved into a full covering position on the
centre-half.

4-2-4 SYSTEM (*fig.* 57)

Reference has already been made to the 4-2-4 system, the double
centre-half play described above is the defensive base upon which
this system is developed.

In mid-field the link between defence and attack is established
by one of the inside-forwards together with one wing half-back.
When the opposing team has the ball these two link men retreat
quickly to become half-backs. When their own team has possession
of the ball they both become supporting inside-forwards. In a rigid
form this sytem of play demands a very high work rate from the
two mid-field or link players. In all phases of the game they work
in close support of each other.

In *fig.* 57 where red team is attacking on its left flank, the IL has
moved into a close supporting position, with the other link man

(RH) affording additional support. These two players give the same support wherever the attacking play develops. In the opposing team, using the same system of play, it may be seen how the two link players assume the defensive roles of half-backs. In this case they are the RH and the IL.

The work demanded from the link players is heavy if the system is a rigid one. Where players are basically competent in most aspects of the game it is possible to share the load from time to time by developing an interchange in function between the two link players and the two central attackers. In the same way the more advanced of the two centre-backs can occasionally see an opportunity to support or exploit an attacking possibility.

In *fig.* 58 one of the link men has an opportunity to run into an

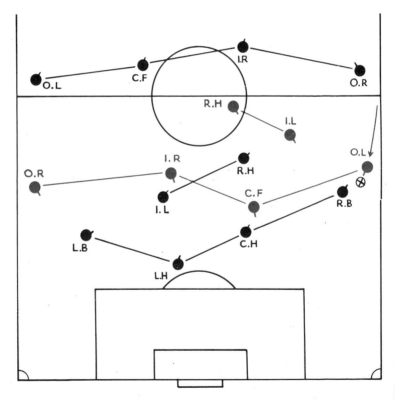

Figure 57

advanced attacking position to receive a pass. The CF seeing this moves away from an advanced position to assume the duties of a link man together with his IL. These interchanges of position are a most important principle of attacking play. Before they can be developed successfully, however, all players must fully understand the duties and responsibilities of all the other members of the team. Interchange of position is not carried out mechanically but is at its most effective when opportunities can be seen and taken as play develops. In the same way the resumption of normal positions should also occur as the development of play demands it.

The basic idea of the 4-2-4 system is to enable a side to have six attacking players, at least, when in possession of the ball and seven defensive players, at least, when the opponents have possession. Tactical variations take place to an increasing extent. In many countries the defensive formation involves a double bank of four defenders.

Both wingers may be required to make the first challenge on their opposing winger should play develop on that side of the field. In *fig.* 59, where play is developing against the left flank of his defence, black OL is challenging the opposing OR while the LB assumes a

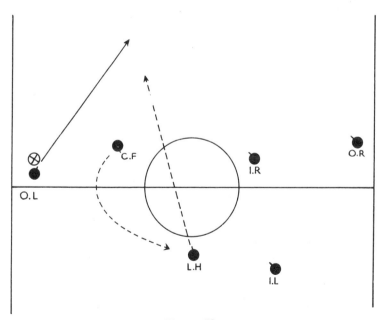

Figure 58

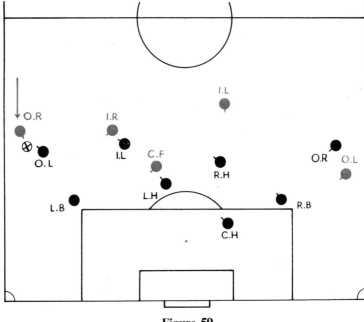

Figure 59

covering role. On the opposite side of the field, black OR has moved back towards the opposing OL to threaten any attempt to play in that direction. In this 'blanket' defence it may be noticed how the front curtain of four defenders tends to slide across the field as the direction of attack changes and how the rear curtain tends to slide in the opposite or covering direction. Many people deplore heavy defensive organization but it is an acknowledgement of the necessity for a team to operate as a single unit and not as two separate halves. Where large numbers of players are committed to rigid defensive positions for most of the time, however, this is unimaginative and negative. From strong defensive positions, attacking play can be applied by using full-backs as attacking units.

In *fig.* 60 we see a run made by a red full-back inside or, more usually, outside his own winger (OR) from a supporting position. The use of defenders running into penetrating positions from behind their attack is an attempt to establish attacking strength.

In any system of play, attacking football can be emphasized by sending players from deep or mid-field positions to support play or indeed to press home the attack. The use of surprise moves is an integral part of successful attacking football but it involves the

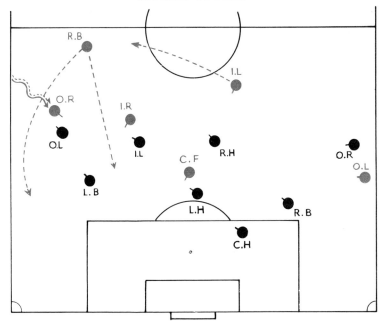

Figure 60

calculation of risk. Risk is calculated on the basis of the under-standing which exists between all the players in a team and, naturally. the state of any particular game.

1-4-1-4 SYSTEM

This system of play is a modification of 4-2-4 in two ways. Defen-sively, strength is increased by withdrawing both wing half-backs to mark the two central attackers in the opposing side. The cover-ing back (CH) in *fig.* 61 is responsible for covering duties across the whole of the field thus enabling both full-backs to mark opposing wingers tightly. The principal mid-field player is now one of the inside-forwards (red IL in *fig.* 61). When possession is regained this mid-field player is supported by one or more of the three central defenders (RH, LH, CH). Provided that the players are basically competent, there is no reason why the full-backs should not also involve themselves in attacking movements since they will frequently find themselves in advanced positions.

The defensive aspect of this system of play is emphasized when

63

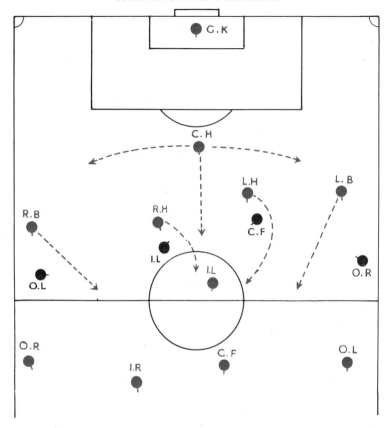

Figure 61

the half-backs and full-backs are restricted to a defensive function. This happens, for example, when the five defenders never, or seldom, advance beyond the half-way line. Here the forward line operates without any support from the rear other than that which can be offered by the forward line itself. To fill the gap between defence and attack, one or two forwards have to take up positions behind the remainder which, of course, means that the likelihood of penetration is still further reduced. Where two teams adopt the same kind of defensive structure we find the worst possible development of negative play.

4-3-3 SYSTEM

A further modification of the 4-2-4 system occurs when a team uses

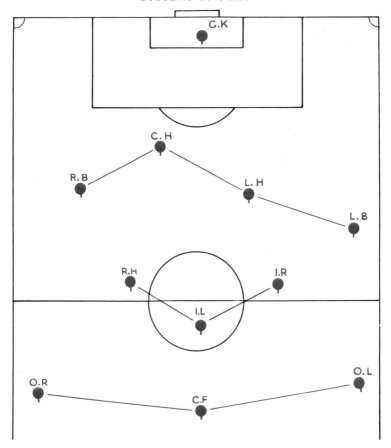

Figure 62

the double centre-half or centre-back system and supports this with a unit of three mid-field players. In *fig*. 62 the mid-field link is maintained by using one wing half-back (RH) and both inside-forwards. These three players form the first bank of the defence and also support the attack at all times. Since the system uses an additional forward in a semi-defensive position it is defensively biased when it is rigidly employed. Attacking play can be em-phasized by allowing the three mid-field players to take part in attacking movements and also by encouraging any of the four backs to break out from defence in support of attacking play whenever they see the opportunity.

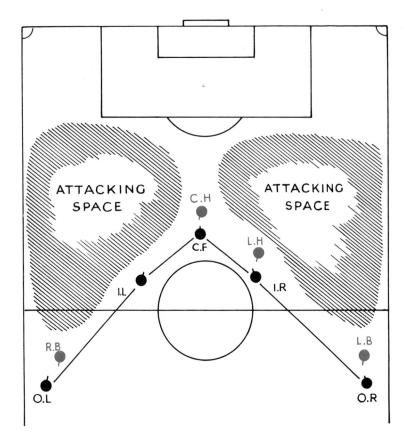

Figure 63

ARROW-HEAD FORMATION

A considerable re-think of defensive systems was caused by the introduction of double centre-forward play. Here, as we have seen, two central attackers were used to upset the rigid function of the stopper centre-half. A similar method has been used to upset the defensive strength of the four-back system where it uses a double centre-half unit as its foundation. Both wingers are withdrawn into mid-field positions and three attackers are sent into advanced striking positions against the two centre-halves (*fig.* 63).

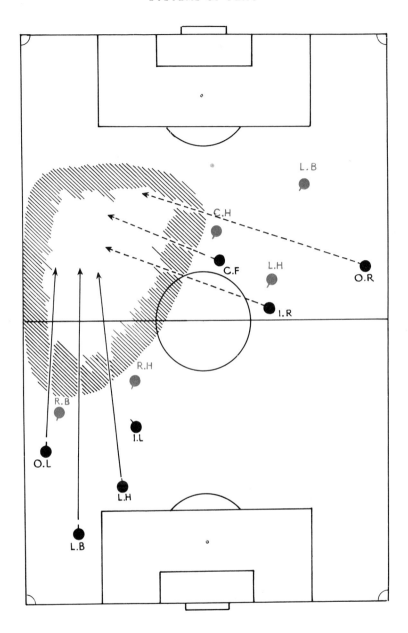

Figure 64

The wingers are used as link players and attacking play is built up on them in order to attract the opposing full-backs as far away from goal as possible. The attack then uses the space which has been left behind the full-backs. Where two of the central attackers remain in fairly central positions, the third attacker can move across the field in search of space behind the full-backs. This plan involves sending attackers towards defenders in order to threaten them. In the past, attacking play was based upon the belief that all attackers should endeavour to get away from defenders. This is good so long as the attackers move towards goal or across the field in trying to escape the attention of defenders. When, too frequently, they move towards their own goal defenders are happy to see them do so since they (the defenders) are in a position to watch play developing in front of them.

A similar development has taken place using one winger as the link player in a very deep position. This system, where the attack is disposed in an echelon formation, has been used with success against the three-back diagonal system of defence.

In *fig.* 64 the deep winger (OL) is frequently the focus of defensive clearances and is supported by the LH, the IL and, if necessary, the LB. Where the opposing RB is drawn into an advanced position and the CH and LB pivot behind him in the diagonal system, a considerable space is left behind the RB and the CH. The ball is played into the space and one or more of the three advance forwards move into the space in an attempt to break the balance of the defence. Alternatively, the attack may be built up on the right hand side of the field by the use of long cross-field passes. The build up is playing on a situation where the attack is equal in number to the defence. Where a defending team is over concerned with marking opposing players on a man-for-man basis, this system has been quite successful. As an answer it has been found that the full-back (RB in *fig.* 65) must be withdrawn to command attacking space and the responsibility for the deep-lying OL is given to the opposing red winger on the same side of the field.

In *fig.* 65 the OR is restricting the source of supply, the deep-lying OL, and the RB has retreated to restrict the possibilities for the receivers.

SLIDING DEFENCES *(The bolt systems)*

Reference was made earlier to the problems involved when defences are required to swing from one side of the field to the other in order to meet opposing attacking threats. This pivoting can be slow and cumbersome although effective when an opposing team concentrates on building up its attacks on the wings. Where an opposing

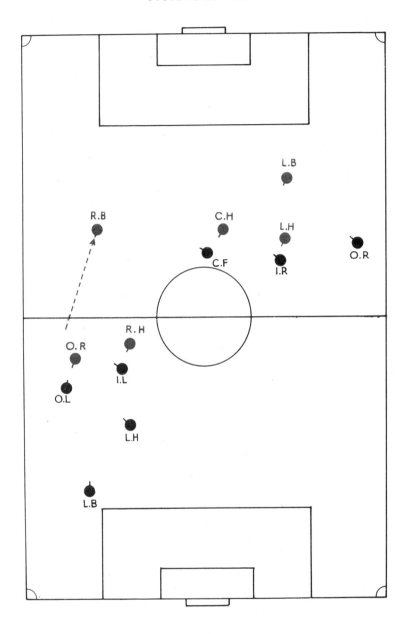

Figure 65

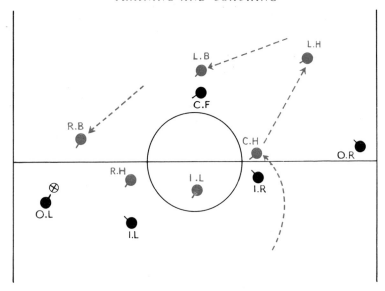

Figure 66

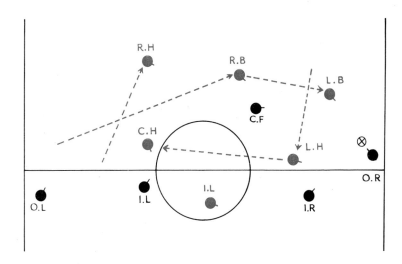

Figure 67

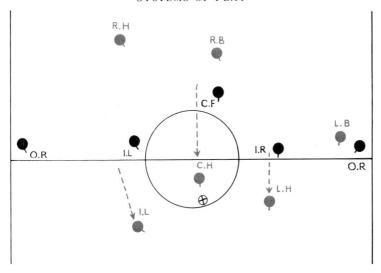

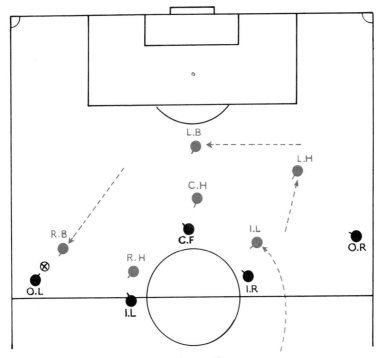

Figure 69

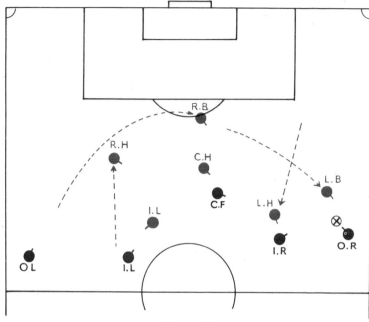

Figure 70

side builds up attacking movements on central players, the pivoting system can be exposed in a square position. Frequent attempts have been made to slide defensive players across the field as a counter to this.

In *fig*. 66 a team is using the CH as a mid-field player or virtually as a wing half-back. Play is developing on the defending RB's side of the field and thus the RB is in close attendance upon the opposing OL. The defending LB has moved across to the CH position and the defending LH has assumed the position of covering full-back. The CH and the RH together with whichever of the inside-forwards is used, form the mid-field unit in defence.

If play should develop on the opposite side of the field the defence will swing accordingly (*fig*. 67). In the event of the red team beginning an attack of its own down the left side of the field, the LH would forsake his full-back position and support the CH and the IL. The LB would assume the orthodox left-back position, the RB would move into the central defensive position and the RH would move into the covering full-back rôle (*fig*. 68).

A similar although more defensively-biased system employs the orthodox stopper centre-half. In *fig*. 69 the covering full-back (LB)

72

has moved into a full central covering position behind the CH. He has become a second centre-half. The LH has withdrawn to become a covering full-back and the IL has become a defensive mid-field player along with the RH.

When play moves across the field the cover reverses its positions (*fig*. 70). The RB becomes a second centre-half, the RH assumes the rôle of covering full-back and the IL drops back to link up with the LH as the mid-field players. The LB has resumed an orthodox full-back position. These systems of play demand a high degree of understanding from the players involved.

In all aspects of defensive play it is necessary for defenders to be able to judge when to mark a player closely and when to fall away from him. Similarly the interchange of positions which a good attack will use requires that the defenders shall be adept at 'passing-on' opposing attackers. As an attacker moves into a defender's zone in defence he is tightly marked. As the attacker moves from one zone to another, different defenders accept the responsibility of marking him.

We have already seen how modern attacking football requires forwards to have a facility for interchanging in order to draw defenders out of position. Similarly we have seen how defensive players can move from defence into positions where they can support attack. This tendency will increase, given the all-round competence of players to understand and take part in aspects of play with which they are not normally familiar. It is no use to expect a full-back to involve himself in attacking movements if he lacks the ball control of a forward. In the same way, for a winger to take the place of a wing half-back is a waste of time if the winger does not fully understand what is required of him at wing half-back. It follows that if players are brought up as specialists, tactical possibilities must be limited. This is not to say that specialization is bad, but in the early stages a player must develop an all-round competence in and understanding of the game as a whole. The more a high degree of specialization is encouraged the more the game is being split up into parts, rendering it less fluid and much more prone to domination by defensive tactics.

73

3 Modern Tactical Development

Tactics are modifications or adaptations of play within a team system and they will be affected by the following considerations.

1. Skills of the individual players in the team.
2. Deficiency of skills in the individual team players.
3. Skills of the opposing players.
4. Lack of skills in the opposing players.
5. Ground and climatic conditions.
6. Injuries to one's own players and to opposing players.
7. The degree of understanding within a team (for example, use of rehearsed movements during play and particularly at throw-in, free-kick, corner-kick, etc.).
8. The state of the game.

Let us look at some examples of the way in which tactics can be affected by the above considerations. Let us imagine that our wingers are both clever ball-players who are capable of beating opponents with the ball but who are not fast runners either with the ball or without it. Tactically, therefore, we shall modify our system of play to make the most of these players' skill with the ball and to disguise their lack of speed. Long passes over the opposing full-backs will be a waste of time except where the wingers have tempted the full-backs into positions remote from their goal. These long passes will be made into the space behind the backs for the centre-forward or perhaps one of the inside-forwards, to run onto. During attacking phases of the game we may decide that the wingers can be used to the greatest advantage nearest to the opponents' penalty-area. If we are able to pass the ball to them in wide positions in this part of the field we may be able to create a situation where they can use their dribbling ability to beat the opposing full-backs and so to turn the flanks of the defence. In this part of the field we may ask our other attackers to deliberately move away from the wingers in order to draw away covering defenders. Similarly we may find that one of our wingers has a marked ability to beat a full-back by going outside him or 'down the line'. Where this is so we need to ensure that the path down the line is clear of other players.

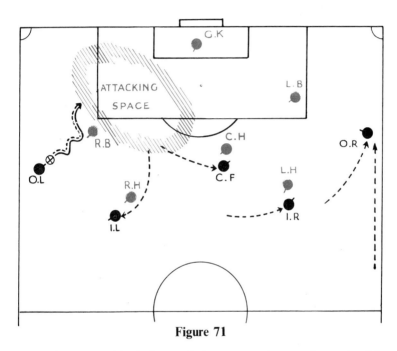

Figure 71

In *fig.* 71 the black forwards have moved away from the OL in such a way as to try to clear the space behind the RB and also to draw defenders away from covering positions. In this way they are helping the OL to establish a position in which he can beat the opposing RB.

In *fig.* 72 where the OL may be capable of beating his full-back on the inside, the other forwards have moved to assist him. The IL has moved behind the RB to the wing (thus maintaining width in attack), trying to draw the RH away from a central covering position. Similarly the other forwards have tried to draw defenders away from the centre part of the field in front of the penalty-area into which the OL must go if he succeeds in beating his full-back. In this way our tactics are being adapted to suit the players' skill, their ability to dribble round opponents, and to disguise their

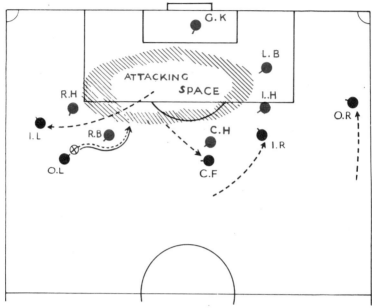

Figure 72

weakness (inability to run fast with and without the ball). A further example of a player's weakness requiring disguise through an adaptation of tactics would arise if our centre-half were not too confident at heading when challenged. This is obviously a serious weakness for a central defensive player. We might require one of the wing half-backs to drop into a covering role behind the centre-half whenever high passes are made in his direction down the centre of the field. Where high crosses are coming from the wings we might arrange for the centre-forward to be marked by one of the wing half-backs with the centre-half adopting a covering position as in *fig.* 73. All that we are doing is trying to make sure that the player is rarely, if ever, in a position where his weakness can be exposed.

During a match we should read certain aspects of the opposing team's play. The general pattern of their play should be recognized

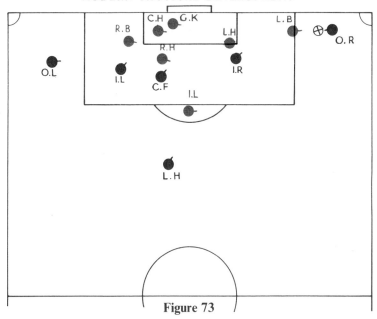

Figure 73

and, after a while, the styles of individual players noted. Tactically, we must exploit their weaknesses. For example, one of the opposing wing half-backs may be inclined to get drawn out to the wing. When the wing-man receives the ball the RH, for example, tends to challenge him if he is near enough. An attempt to exploit this weakness tactically might involve our IL moving out to extreme wing positions both behind and in front of the OL.

In *fig.* 74 the IL has moved behind the OL and the RH can challenge the OL, as he is inclined to do, since he can see both the IL and the OL. In doing so he is leaving a large space in the centre of the field. The RB dare not come forward to fill this gap since he will leave the RH uncovered. If, by good understanding, either of the two wing half-backs can read this situation, they can make a quick break into this dangerous space. By being drawn away from a central defensive position the RH is ignoring the principles of defensive play. Other forwards have assisted by 'moving off the ball', to draw defenders from covering positions.

Frequently, it is difficult to spot weaknesses in an opposing side and in these circumstances it may be necessary to direct our attention to their strongest aspects of play. A team is confident in doing the things it can do well. To play on the strength of a team is to try to encourage it to become over-confident.

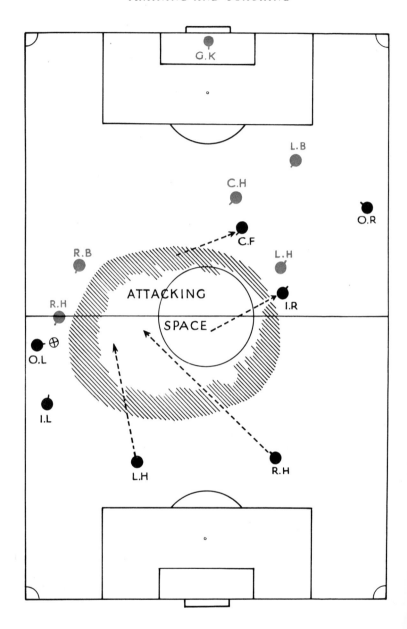

Figure 74

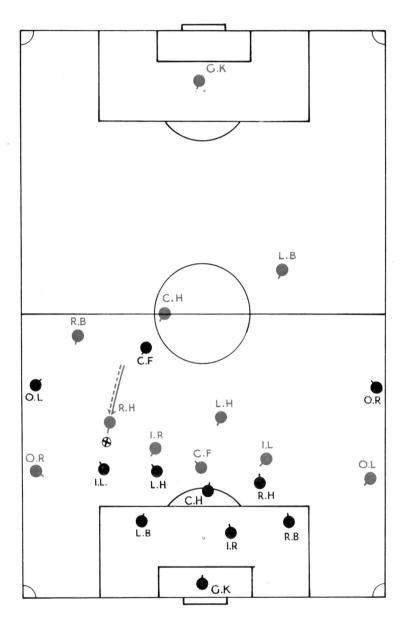

Figure 75

Let us imagine ourselves up against players who are showing themselves to be a strong attacking side. Individually and collectively they are quick and accurate and possess clever dribblers; also they can shoot. We might decide to encourage them to attack by falling back or retreating to the edge of our penalty-area where we set up a defensive structure of seven or eight players. Our aim is to draw more and more of the opposing players into attacking movements. Our defensive aim is to restrict the amount of free space within our defence and to restrict the movement of attacking players behind us. When a side is heavily committed to attack, it is most vulnerable to counter-attack since there is the maximum amount of space behind the rearmost defenders (*fig. 75*).

To encourage heavy attacking play we might ask both our inside forwards to adopt deep defensive positions (for example, *fig. 75*)

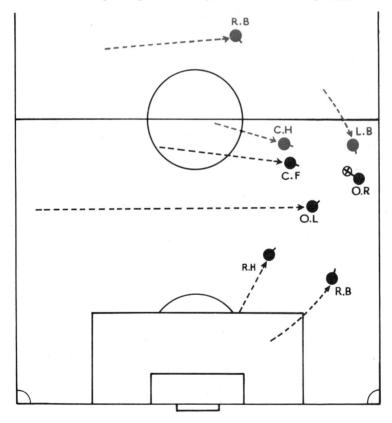

Figure 76

in order to encourage the opposing wing half-backs into advanced attacking movements. If the ball can now be played from defence quickly we have established possession of the ball in a three-against-three situation where our OR, CF, and OL are opposed by the LB, CH, and RB. If our three forwards can support each other quickly a rapid break-through may be achieved. Since both inside-forwards have taken up deep defensive positions when the break is made it must be quickly supported by the nearest defensive players.

In *fig.* 76 the OL and the CF have moved across to the OR to whom a clearance has been made. In order to exploit the quick break through it may be necessary for both the RB and the RH to support this attacking move.

Ground and climatic conditions will obviously affect match tactics considerably. Players with only average ball control are made to look much better than they are on soft grounds. On hard, bumpy grounds and particularly in strong winds the same players are in difficulty. The type of pass to be used will also be affected by different playing conditions. On a firm ground, with a wet top, players can increase the range of their ground passes by as much as twenty-five yards. On a very soft ground the range of effective ground passes is reduced considerably with the added danger of the ball sticking half way to its target. It should be no surprise to find many teams playing better football against a strong wind than with the wind behind them. Against the wind the ball has to be kept low and therefore players are often forced to support each other rather more closely. When playing with the wind there is a temptation to let the passes go more freely with the result that forward players tend to remain in more advanced positions. This causes the team to become stretched and often a gap appears between the 'feeders' and the 'chasers'.

Here are other sets of conditions which can affect basic team play. On a wet but firm ground where the greasy top surface allows the ball to skid through easily, defenders are in trouble when they are made to turn. This means that the ball can be pushed through to attacking players with a great degree of accuracy and a greater range of passing distance. At the same time the use of quick, square passing in attack can cause difficulties for the attacking side since the slightest inaccuracy will cause the receiver to have to turn under extreme difficulties. Building-up play should be to the receiver's feet and preferably forwards or backwards rather than square. In this way the receiver is moving on to the ball and is able to assess the passing possibilities in front of him with the minimum of difficulty. Defensively, these ground conditions will mean that defen-

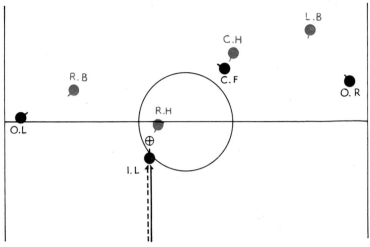

Figure 77

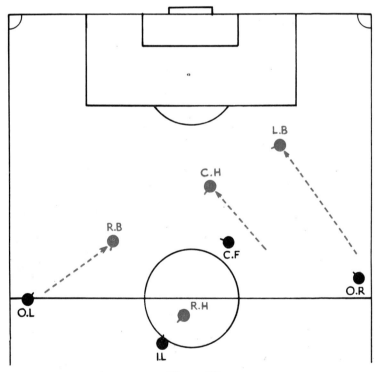

Figure 78

ders will not be able to commit themselves so readily to interceptions or to tight marking positions. They will tend to take up positions well inside their opponents' in order to avoid the increased possibility of passes going through the defence on the inside of players.

In *fig*. 77 where ground conditions are firm, the RB is near to the opposing OL in order to try to intercept a pass from the IL or to make a quick tackle. The LB has assumed an orthodox covering position. The defenders can take up these positions because they know that ground conditions will allow them to turn quickly should the necessity arise.

In *fig*. 78, where playing conditions are treacherous, the RB has deliberately stood off the OL to narrow the gap between the RH and himself. Similarly the CH has moved over into a tighter covering position and the LB has swung over to offer maximum cover to the CH. They have done this to prevent the possibility of passes being made behind and between them.

When playing against the wind, teams must support each other more closely in defence in order to cover against the possibility of the wind causing the ball to play tricks. In attacking play, therefore, considerable use may be made of the low, powerfully driven pass through the opposing defence. A ball so delivered is held by the wind thus giving advanced attackers a better chance of catching the pass.

When playing with the wind the passing range of all the players is increased through wind assistance. Cross-field passes are much more effective but down-field passes have to be measured carefully because they may run away from attackers too quickly. The chip pass is effective under these conditions since it is delivered with a minimum amount of forward movement and the height achieved allows the wind to carry the ball thus causing difficulty to defenders.

When playing with a strong wind players tend to forget the principle of supporting the player with the ball. This is a major fault whatever the conditions. Possibly one of the most embarrassing and difficult situations in which to play is that produced by a bright sun just before it sets. In these circumstances attacking teams will deliberately build up play so that passes into dangerous parts of the field are delivered with the sun shining from behind the passes. This means that it shines into the eyes of defending players. On any away ground it is worth finding out:

1. Which way the prevailing wind blows
2. From which direction the sun shines at various times during the afternoon.

Both minor and major injuries are to be expected in a game and they are part and parcel of the game. As such they must seriously affect not only tactics but the basic system of play. So far as injuries to one's own team are concerned there are certain basic rules which apply:

1. If a player cannot move about with a fair degree of freedom he should not remain on the field. The long term consequences of a further aggravation of an injury do not warrant risks being taken.
2. Where the injury is of a minor nature the player should be used in a position in which he will cause the maximum trouble to the opposing team.

Some people advocate moving an injured player to the wing where he will be least involved in play. If this is the argument then by the same token he will cause the least trouble to the opposing side and, at the same time, he will unbalance attacking play. If he is moved to the centre-forward position he cannot be ignored by the opposition, and, at the same time, passes can be made to him which enable him to *pass the ball to* other players with the least possible inconvenience. The attack also has the best possible balance under these circumstances. Different minor injuries affect a player's playing performance in different ways. Leg injuries make running, quick starting, and kicking difficult. Injuries to the hips and lower back make twisting and turning difficult. Obviously, recognition of these factors will cause the opposing team to try to make the injured player do whatever is most difficult by playing on his weakness. It may be thought that the tactical exploitation of an injured player is morally wrong. Extended to a logical conclusion this would mean that any game in which a player has been injured should be replayed when the sides are of equal strength. Any player who stays on the field when he has been injured does so with the aim of playing a part in team play to the best of his capabilities. One side must aim to use his limitations to advantage, the other side must expose these limitations. These factors not apparently directly concerned with the game of football have to be recognized in tactical adaptation.

One of the most important aspects of tactical development involves establishing a numerical advantage. Whether in attack or defence, a team must aim at having at least one extra man. In attack this will mean that however tight the marking by opposing defenders, one man is free to support or press home the advantage. It may be that the numerical superiority refers to a brief moment in time and a small space in which two attackers are able to interpass and beat one defender. The same superiority may be established during a full attacking movement which is supported from a deep defensive position. A full-back may suddenly join in an advanced attacking movement for example. In defence the extra man may be involved in deflecting the opposing attack across the field to less dangerous areas or he may be responsible for covering gaps rather than for marking specific opposing players.

Whatever the phase of the game a numerical advantage must be the aim and once it has been established its exploitation depends upon one thing alone: accuracy in passing. It has often been said that if a player cannot pass accurately and with control he cannot really play football. Certainly, all the possibilities for combined tactical play depend to a great extent upon this technique. The ability to direct a pass exactly where it is intended to go, at the right speed, with just enough spin or swerve if they are required, is of major importance to all players from the goalkeeper to the outside left.

Where we are concerned with the exploitation of numerical superiority irrespective of the actual number of players involved, what we are really concerned with is the establishment and exploitation of a two-against-one situation.

Figure 79

In *fig.* 79 where six players are defending against six attackers the movement of the LH in close support of his OL has, in that phase of wing play, created a two-against-one situation. In other words although the total numbers are equal, momentarily, a numerical advantage has been established. This situation can be created if nearby players are willing to support the player who is in possession of the ball.

SUPPORTING OR ZONING ON THE BALL

Whenever a player receives the ball he should have already assessed the situation around him and he should have made a selection from the passing opportunities available. A good player will read the game wherever the ball may be and however unlikely it seems that he will be involved in play immediately. In this way he tries to be one, two, or three moves ahead all the time. He may receive the ball when rapid changes of play are happening and there is much movement of players around him. In these 'tight' situations he may not have time to make accurate and controlled judgements. Obviously, therefore, if he has one player to whom he can pass he has no choice. If he has three or four the position is simplified for him. These choices can only be possible if players move towards the player towards whom the ball is being played rather than away from him. One often hears the expression 'they had the luck or the run of the ball'. It is only possible for a team to have the run of the ball if that team has sufficient players there to whom the ball can run. This movement of supporting players towards the man with the ball achieves two things. It simplifies his choice of passing possibilities and also draws opponents in the same direction. This in itself assists the player with the ball. If, for example, he had decided on a long forward pass, zoning on the ball causes opponents to be drawn away from marking and covering positions. Thus his long pass may have an enhanced chance of success.

SETTING-UP PLAY

A team which plays controlled, methodical football will often employ deliberate passing movements which appear to have little or no purpose so far as scoring goals is concerned. They may deliberately interpass to draw opponents towards the ball. They do this in order to create openings for a through-pass towards their opponents' goal.

In *fig.* 80 the IR has passed to the CF moving towards him and who is being tightly marked by the CH. The CF then gives a return pass at an angle and turns away from the centre of the field. The pass has been set up with the intention of drawing the CH away

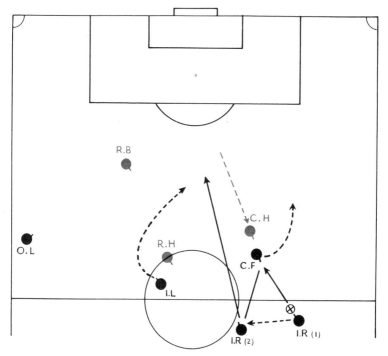

Figure 80

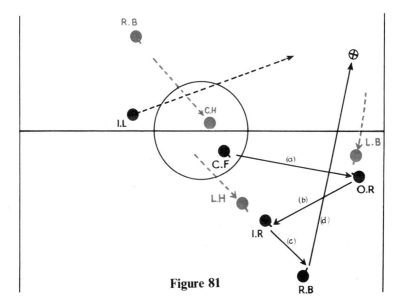

Figure 81

from his goal in order that a through-pass can be given into the space behind him.

In *fig.* 81 the IR, the CF, and the OR have all interpassed while moving towards their right-back. These setting-up passes have been aimed at drawing the opposing LH, CH, and LB down-field to create space into which the RB may play the ball, perhaps for the IL who moves off on a diagonal run behind these opposing defenders. The higher the class of football the more a team must use setting-up to tempt the opposing team into making mistakes. One of the aspects of football which is of vital importance and yet, because it is based upon human weaknesses, is most difficult to calculate, is that involving ball possession. If a team is submitted to long periods of play in which it is denied possession of the ball, its players become anxious and take risks in trying to regain possession. At this time such a team is most vulnerable to quick counter-attack.

KEEP BALL

A recent development in top-class play has been the use of interpassing play of an apparently purposeless nature. Here a team with a commanding lead will interpass the ball in any direction and often backwards in order to slow the game down and make their opponents advance to try to regain possession. The losing team is obliged to take risks to regain possession. Its players must commit themselves to chasing the ball and opposing players. This means that players can be drawn into bad positions and that space is created between and behind defensive positions. Obviously in these circumstances a quick counter-attack has an enhanced chance of success. Denying one's opponents possession of the ball is an important skill and demands team work of a very high order.

SQUARE PASSING

When used properly this can be an excellent means of drawing defenders. If it develops generally, however, it involves considerable risks and can lead to negative play.

In *fig.* 82 the LH and RH have interpassed square across the field with the object of drawing the opposing IR and IL into a square position. This is a position in which they are not covering each other. At the same time, they are easily exposed for a through-pass. Square passing becomes negative when players use it as a first choice, in other words when they are always looking for the easy pass. This may be for two reasons. Firstly, they have got into

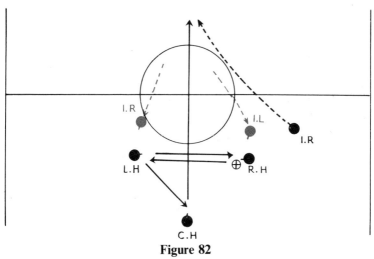

Figure 82

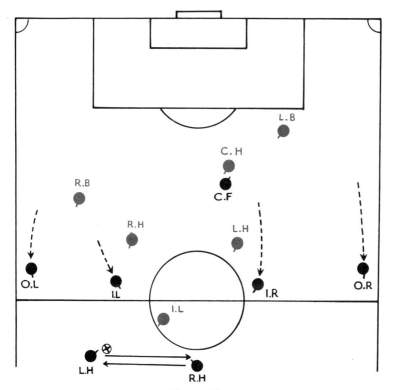

Figure 83

the bad habit of not wishing to accept the responsibility for making a through pass which might be intercepted. Secondly, they may have been forced into this sort of play because other players will not take up forward positions where they may be strongly challenged.

In *fig.* 83 all the black forwards with the exception of the CF want to move away from the defenders thus the LH and RH have very few opportunities to make penetration passes. This will cause interpassing movements to become negative.

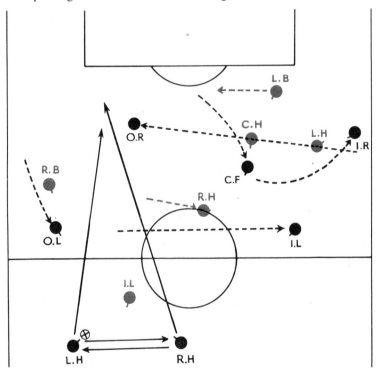

Figure 84

In *fig.* 84 where the OR has made a positive forward movement which has been assisted by the diagonal movements of the CF and IR, there are opportunities for progressive, purposeful play. What is known as 'front running' demands a great deal of effort and considerable courage. Forward runs take players into dangerous positions and, naturally, positions in which they are likely to be tightly marked and submitted to strong physical challenge. Without front runners a team has little or no chance of effecting penetration. One will see a great deal of pretty interpassing all to no purpose.

DIAGONAL RUNNING

Reference has already been made to the need for interchange of positions in attack. Mobility in attack is a fundamental principle of the game. Any good defence will rarely, if ever, allow attacking players to run unopposed towards goal. The more that these long, through-passes are attempted, the more a defence will fall back, cover and so cut off the possibility. The higher the class of football, the more this is true. If players insist in always running towards goal they are making themselves difficult targets for a pass and they are also taking defenders in a direction which the defenders are most happy to take (*fig.* 85). In the diagram one can see the

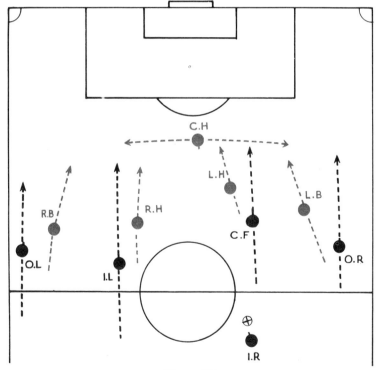

Figure 85

difficulty which faces the IR in passing to any of the other forwards particularly where the opposing team is using a sweeper centre half. The forwards who are running towards goal are helping the defence to reduce the space into which the IR wants to pass the ball. Moreover since they are running away from him the forwards are making an accurate pass extremely difficult.

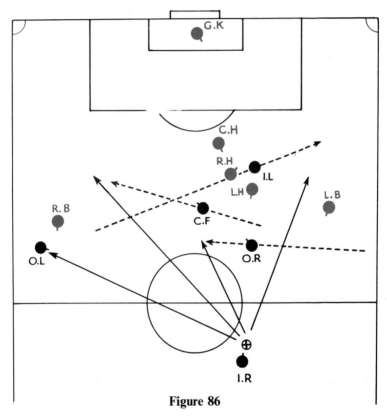

Figure 86

The diagonal movements of the forwards pose a different problem. To what extent dare the defenders now fall back and leave men unmarked? The purpose of diagonal running is to cause defenders to react by moving across the field. Better passing angles are made for the player with the ball and gaps are created through which he can pass. At the same time defenders are discouraged from retreating to reduce the space behind them. Many of these runs must be made, some of which are carried out with the intention of receiving a pass, others are undertaken to create better passing possibilities for other players. In *fig.* 86 the movement of the IL from an ortho-dox IL position through positions behind the opposing left-half and left-back is an example of moving in such a way. The player's main aim is to attract the attention of opposing players and if possible to draw them some of the way with him. If, for example, the RH follows him part of the way a gap has thus been opened for the CF's diagonal run into a much more dangerous position.

MOVEMENT OFF THE BALL

The kind of running movements which have just been referred to are known as 'movements off the ball'. Moving off the ball is required of all players in as much as they must always be aware of the need to help the player in possession by making decoy move-

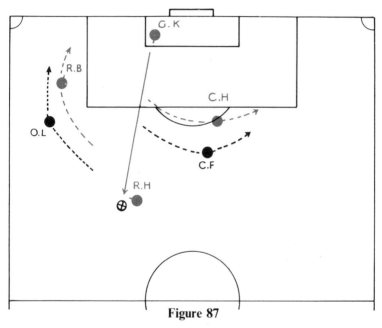

Figure 87

ments. A simple example might be that shown in *fig.* 87. At this goal-kick both the CH and the RB can see that their RH is in a good position for a pass. The opposing OL and CF, however, are too near to the line of the pass to make it worth the risk. Seeing this the defenders both move away, calling for a pass at the same time. If they attract the opposing OL and CF with them they clear the path for a goal-kick to the RH. If the opposing players are not drawn then they themselves, the RB and the CH, are available for

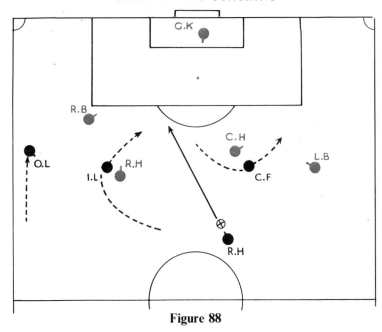

Figure 88

the goal-kick to be passed to them.

Another example might be that shown in *fig.* 88. Here the CF has turned away from a central position trying to draw the CH with him. By so doing he is trying to open up the line of a pass from the RH to the IL. The OL would also help by moving fairly steadily towards the corner flag trying to attract the attention of the RB. His aim would be to keep the full-back's attention away from his covering duty in the centre of the field. The movements of the CF and the OL are good examples of movement off the ball since, in both cases, should the RH not feel able to make a pass to the IL, these two players are still in a position to receive a pass themselves. The aim of this sort of play is to put a defender or defenders in two minds and, ideally, to try to ensure that whichever choice the defender makes he is wrong.

In *fig.* 88 the centre-half can either stay to block the run of the IL or he can cover the CF. If he fails to do the former an immediate path to goal is open. If he lets the CF go then the CF may receive an effective pass. This is an excellent example of the extent to which the calculation of risk is an important skill. A decision has to be made in a split second if the runs of the attacking players are well timed.

94

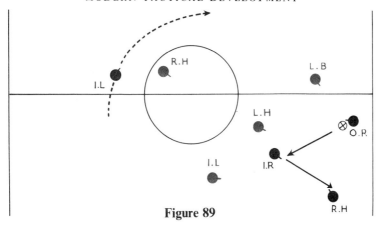

Figure 89

BLIND SIDE PLAY

We have already seen how some players tend to become 'ball watchers'. They are easily distracted from their defensive duties within the defensive organisation by the player with the ball. One result of this is that it allows opposing attackers to move on to the defender's blind-side (*fig.* 89).

In this diagram the RH has lost sight of the opposing IL by having his attention drawn to the interplay between the opposing RH, IR and OR. This has allowed the IL to move past him on the side nearest to the goal. At all times when defending, players should try to position themselves in such a way as to see nearby attackers and the ball at the same time.

In *fig.* 90 the LH has been drawn towards the OR and he has allowed the opposing IR to move on to his blind side. The RH

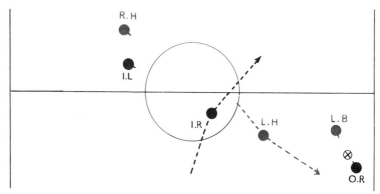

Figure 90

however has positioned himself so that he can watch the ball, the opposing IL, and general play all at the same time. One of the main aims in attacking play is for forwards to get into blind-side positions and particularly behind defenders.

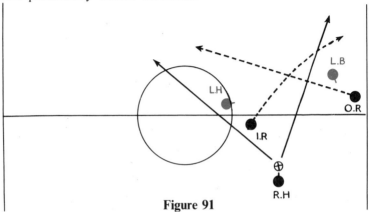

Figure 91

CROSS-OVER PLAYS

These are diagonal runs made to achieve blind-side positions and which are often worked out between two or more players.

In *fig.* 91 the RH has the ball. The IR runs behind the LB and as he does so the OR moves across and behind him into the IR position. Momentarily, the defenders may be taken by surprise and one or both of the attackers may find himself free for a pass from the RH.

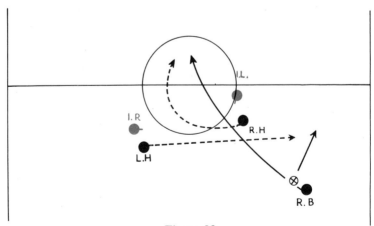

Figure 92

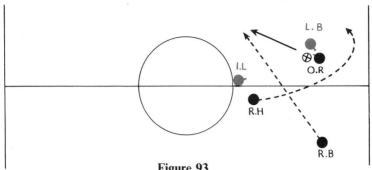

Figure 93

In *fig.* 92 the RH is closely watched by the IL and is not a safe passing possibility for the RB. The LH runs diagonally in front of the IL hoping to take the IR with him. Meanwhile the RH turns and runs diagonally in the opposite direction, perhaps freeing himself for a pass from the RB.

A final example (*fig.* 93) shows the OR being challenged by the opposing LB. The RH is tightly marked but runs to the wing behind the OR taking the IL with him. The RB seeing that the way is now clear runs across the RH for a pass in the inside right position. As with all passing movements the timing of the players' run-

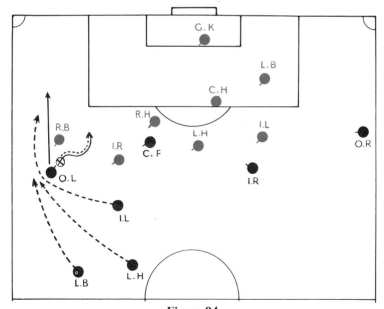

Figure 94

ning movements is of major importance to cause the maximum
disorganization in the opposing defence.

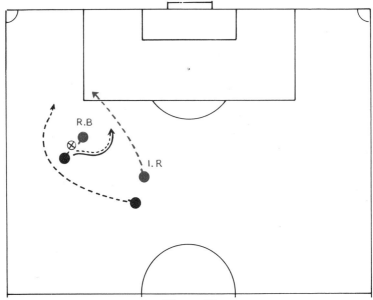

Figure 95

OVERLAPPING RUNS AND RUNS FROM BEHIND ATTACKING PLAYERS

The need for surprise and also for creating situations in which,
numerically, an attacking side has an advantage, are important
aspects of attacking play. Where a defence is well organized, the
defenders will be adept at moving so far to mark attackers and
then leaving them to other defenders. They will also be acutely
conscious of any attempt to move behind them. Overlapping runs
are often used to try to turn the defence, in these circumstances.

In *fig.* 94 the defence is numerically very strong and able to
mark opponents tightly and cover well. To produce an overlap the
OL who is in possession of the ball moves in-field towards the
opposing right-back. The CF and IR move slightly away from the
left-wing principally to reduce the cover on that flank. The overlap
can then be made by either the IL, the LB, or LH running outside
the OL and down the line. The OL can now play the ball down the
wing or, if the RB is clever enough to block this possibility, he can
try to beat the RB on the inside.

If the IR drops back to cover the pass down the wing the way is open for the OL to move inside (*fig.* 95). If the IR attempts to

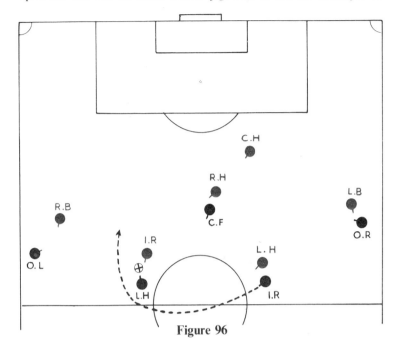

Figure 96

cover this possibility then he must leave the pass down the touch-line as a good possibility. The use of overlapping runs is an excellent way of achieving extra men in tight playing situations and, at the same time, a high degree of mobility in attacking play. The success of this move lies in the fact that opponents do not pay so much attention to a supporting player's movement when it is behind the player with the ball.

In *fig.* 96 the passing possibilities for the LH are very limited, the opposing defence is marking tightly and covering well. Should the IR move away from the opposing LH and behind his own LH, it is unlikely that he will be followed and he may thus produce an overlap position against the IR and, at the same time, possibly expose the opposing RB to a two-against-one situation.

The use of defenders making surprise attacking runs will play an increasing part against heavy defensive systems of play. From deep positions they are able to gather speed over a long distance and they are able to create surprise by choosing their moment when to support the attack.

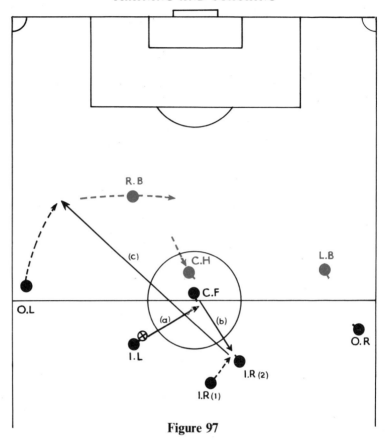

Figure 97

REVERSE PASSING

Defence is concerned with reducing the amount of space through which and into which passes can be made, and also with restricting the scope to move of attacking players. Defence is concerned with setting problems and the responsibility for doing something about this is fairly and squarely on the shoulders of the attacking side. In order to try to create attacking space and at the same time to lull defenders into a false sense of security, the direction of the attack must be changed frequently and rapidly. The reverse pass involves movement of the ball in one direction and a sudden reversal of the direction in which the ball and play generally has been moving.

In *fig.* 97 play has developed from left to right. The IL has passed to the CF who has pushed a pass back to the IR. All these players are moving in the same direction. The defence will tend to move across in the same direction to cover attacking developments on that side of the field. The IR then hits a long reverse pass to the outside-left since defensive pressure has been removed from that flank.

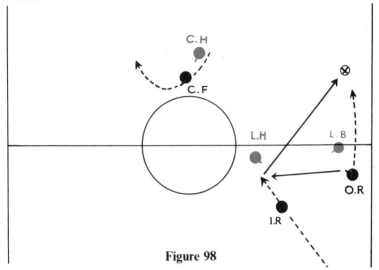

Figure 98

A common situation in which a reverse pass can be used with telling effect is between the wing-man and his inside-forward (*fig.* 98).

Having received a pass from the OR the IR makes ground towards the centre of the field away from his OR. He then makes a reverse pass behind the opposing LB which his OR can run on to. Notice how the CF has assisted by drawing the CH away from a position in which he can cover the LB. This is another example of intelligent movement off the ball.

CHANGING THE PACE OF A GAME

One of the major difficulties involved in playing the traditionally open or long-passing and fast-running game is that it tends to become a one pace game. Since fast, longish passes have to be delivered quickly, inaccuracy is likely to occur. This in turn means that attacking players tend to begin their attacking runs early in order to get a start on opponents. The more inaccurate the pass the earlier they tend to run with the result that the pace of the game becomes faster and hence more inaccurate. This type of football may be exciting to watch but it is a bad risk and when accuracy deteriorates the game becomes a shambles. Long passes are extremely important to good football provided that they are used when the possibility for being accurate and therefore successful is at its greatest.

A team which plays this type of game consistently, quickly attunes the opposing team to its speed. Very little surprise is possible since the pace of the game has little variation. Attacking players are in some difficulty since they have no time themselves in which to read the developments in play which take place behind them. They know that the ball will be delivered quickly and powerfully and that they must be prepared to run early.

Slowing the pace of the game does not necessarily mean that players take more time over movements; this would result in casual play which can lead to people being caught in possession of the ball and to passes being intercepted. Slowing the pace of the game is mainly achieved by changing the direction of play away from the opposing team. Safe passes are made with no immediately apparent intention of penetrating the opposing defence. This achieves the following purposes. There is a number of players near to the ball and therefore any one of these is likely to have time in which to make the penetration pass in a controlled way. Opponents are likely to be deceived into standing still or even into being drawn away from the goal which they are defending. Since there appears to be no immediate threat from the apparently purposeless interpassing their defensive concentration may lapse. Changing the pace of a game is usually achieved by mid-field players and those behind them. This is a relatively safe part of the field since mistakes can be covered, particularly when a group of four or five players is involved in interpassing.

In *fig*. 99 the black team is slowing the game down through static interpassing between OL, LB, LH and IL with the CH, RH, and RB in covering positions and also available to take part in the passing movement if required. Here opposing players may be drawn towards play. There is plenty of space behind the red defenders should any of the black mid-field players see an opportunity for a long penetration pass. Further possibilities would arise if one or two players delivered long passes accurately. It may be, for example, that in *fig*. 99 the LH and the IR are the main users of the long pass. Tactically, therefore, the forwards who are in an advanced position can expect long through-passes whenever the ball is played to one of these two players. The possibility for pre-arranged tactical moves is greatly increased.

Against a diagonal defence, for example, we may use the following tactic based upon the LH's ability to deliver a long accurate

102

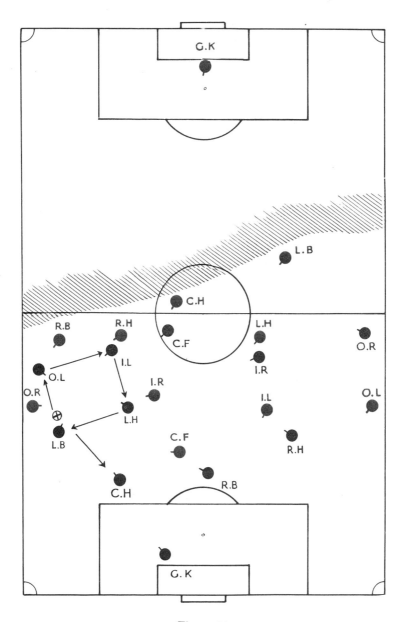

Figure 99

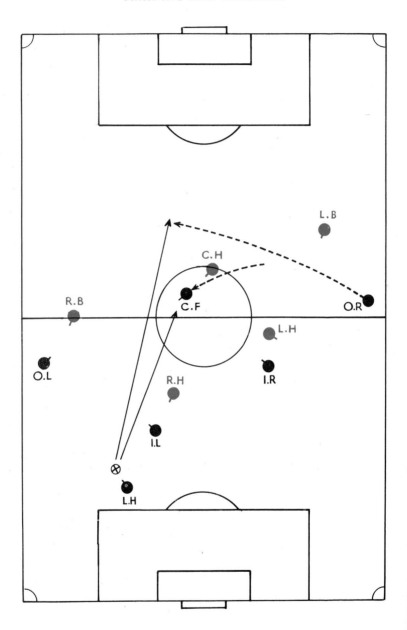

Figure 100

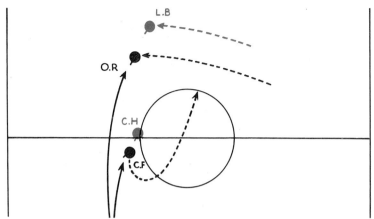

Figure 101

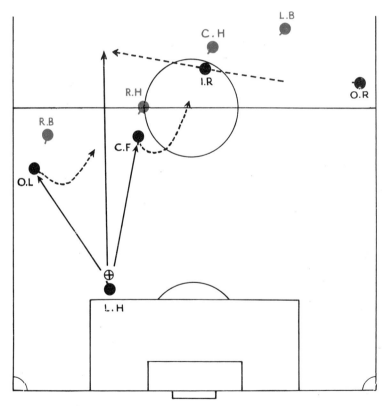

Figure 102

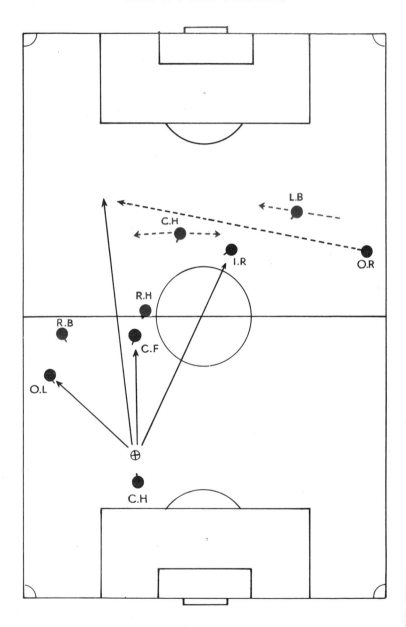

Figure 103

through-pass (*fig.* 100).

In any defensive structure it is important that the attacking side should, as far as possible, prevent the rearmost covering defender from doing his job, which is to cover other defenders. If the OR remains in a deep, wing position the LB can do his job. If, however, by pre-arrangement, the attacking side bases its quick, attacking play on a long pass from the LH, the OR may use a crossfield run in the following way. For any penetration pass there should, if possible, be two alternatives at least. In this situation we may decide that the basic pass shall be a long one from the LH to the feet of the CF who moves into an inside-forward position to receive it. If the OR can time his crossfield run behind the opposing centre-half, then our LH has two possibilities—he can use the basic pass to the CF, or he can lengthen his pass over the CF and the opposing centre-half's head to his OR (*fig.* 101).

In this way we may have freed the OR in an advanced attacking position. If the LB moves across and marks the OR tightly we have succeeded in playing up to a defender behind whom there is no cover and if the CF is quick to turn inside we have created the possibility of a break-through.

In the same way we might use a long passing build up to the OL (*fig.* 102). Here, against a double centre-half system, we have sent one of our forwards onto the covering defender, in this case the CH. This will prevent him from doing his covering job as freely as he would like. This is illustrated in *fig.* 103. Here the IR is only concerned with staying on-side and since the ball and an opponent are in view, this is no problem. The centre-half can only move across into a full covering position behind his RB and RH if he is sure that the IR cannot be reached with a pass. To offset this the LB would, of course, swing over to cover the IR. In this case one could then expect the OR to move across field in search of the through-pass.

These long-passing tactics are only really possible when the deliverer of the final pass has time to be accurate and when the potential receivers of his pass have time to see what is likely to happen. Defenders are at a disadvantage because, while they too can see what is likely to happen, they do not know what their opponents are trying to achieve.

We have already seen how retreat and consolidation are basic principles of defensive play. We also know that defensive football is relatively easy to organize since it is negative. There is nothing basically creative or imaginative about defence. When teams lack creative players, therefore, they will tend to fall back on heavy defensive organization established quickly in the small area in

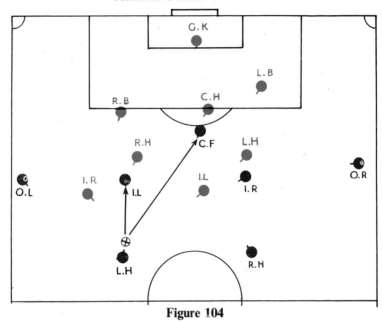

Figure 104

front of goal. Here, an attacking team will find itself unable to break through the opposing defence in mid-field; moreover it will be faced by a large numerical superiority near to goal, making certain tactics necessary.

PLAYING ACCURATELY TO FEET

In the less congested area in mid-field, passes can be delivered in front of a player for him to collect in his stride and often at speed. The same sort of pass is necessary in any forceful attacking move-ment but the nearer the attacking side are to a massed defence, the less will be the scope for making such a pass. Here it becomes vitally important that the build-up of attacking play is by con-trolled passes made to the feet of forwards. Often the receivers of such passes will be in positions with their backs towards their opponents' goal.

In *fig.* 104 one can see the necessity for accuracy and control in the LH's use of the ball. The passes to the IL and the CF must be made to their feet and with just enough pace to ensure that they are not intercepted. Passes delivered with too much pace will be difficult to control by a player who is tightly marked. At the same time, the ability to play to the feet of tightly marked players is important here. Defenders must mark tightly by moving close to

108

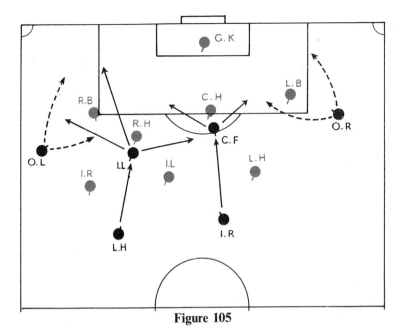

Figure 105

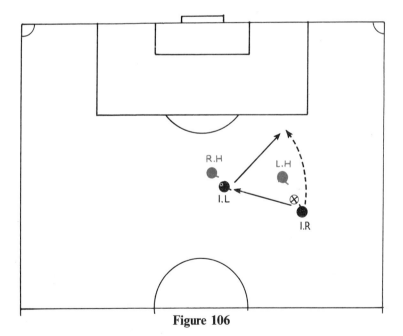

Figure 106

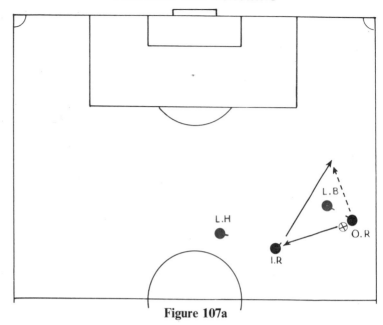

Figure 107a

the opposing forward; if they do not, they may give him time to control the ball and shoot for goal. If the player to whom the ball is played can control it while using his body as a shield, then there is the possibility for a pass to be pushed or flicked away to on-coming attackers. In this way we are using the forward players as rebound surfaces.

SCREENING

This is a technique which is used whereby the body is used to screen the ball from an opponent when the ball is actually in a player's possession or when it comes within playing distance. Against tight marking opponents it is a very necessary skill since it enables a player to hold the ball or to hide his intentions so far as passing the ball is concerned.

We can see how the attacker moves in front of the defender so that his body is always between the defender and the line of the pass. It he is skilled at deflecting the approach pass to other for-wards, shooting opportunities can be created (*fig.* 105).

THE WALL PASS

The pass which is deflected by a player who is screening the ball

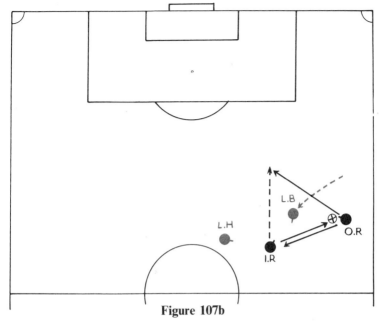

Figure 107b

has been likened to the pass a player is returned after kicking a ball against a wall. The angle at which the ball rebounds will vary according to the angle of the pass. The wall pass is often used to exploit a situation where, momentarily, two players are facing one opponent. Alternatively, as in *fig*. 106, where one player is able to pass the ball to a tightly-marked colleague screening the ball from their opponent and returns it at an angle between the two defenders. Many different uses of the wall pass can be practised to suit various situations.

In *fig*. 107a the orthodox wall pass is given from the IR to the OR who runs behind the LB. In *fig*. 107b LB has moved to cut off this pass and the IR has given a return pass to the OR who now acts as the wall. He pushes the ball at an angle behind the full-back for the IR to run through. The essential factors in a successful wall passing movement are that the player who acts as the wall should be in a position where his partner can make the first pass to him. Secondly, the 'wall' player should be either standing still or moving sideways towards his partner and thirdly, that the return or wall pass should be given first time. The wall pass is executed quickly but it is most effectively employed when the approach play has been slowed down. The change of pace in interpassing movements is a most important technique.

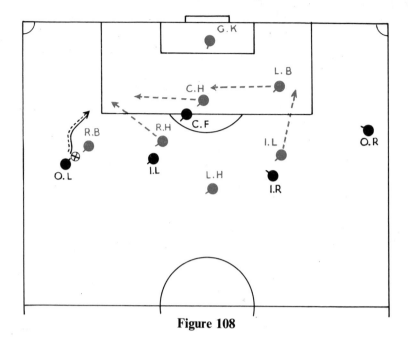

Figure 108

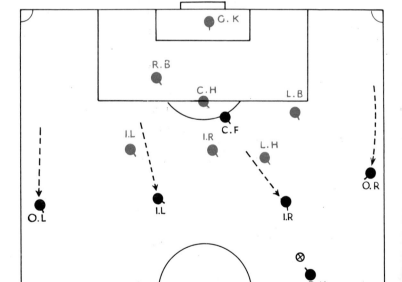

Figure 109

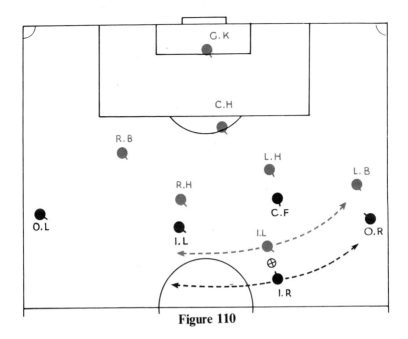

Figure 110

DRIBBLING AND COMMITTING DEFENDERS

Football today is an organized and planned game at the very highest levels. While systems of play and tactics are always changing, the extent to which organization can be the basis of success depends on the skill, understanding, and techniques which are brought to the game by individual players. Thus the technique of beating an opponent by dribbling past him is of ever-increasing importance. Players who are capable of taking on opposing players and beating them are capable of causing confusion and chaos in the best-organized defences.

If in the situation (*fig.* 108) the OL can beat the RB, he will cause other defensive players to leave their normal marking positions to try to cover the break-through. This will cause other forwards to be left free. In the past a great deal of emphasis has been placed on attacking players finding open spaces away from defenders. In the modern game these spaces are increasingly difficult to find since defences are more intensely organized. A defending team will often allow the opposing attackers to find space away from the goal but the nearer to goal attackers move the more space is denied to them.

In *fig.* 109 where the forwards move towards the RH, who has the ball, they may be allowed a fair amount of space. Where they move towards the goal they will find space denied by the concen-

113

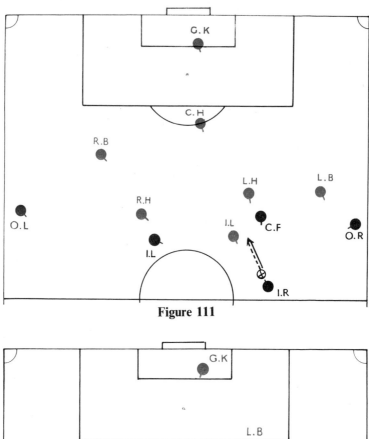

Figure 111

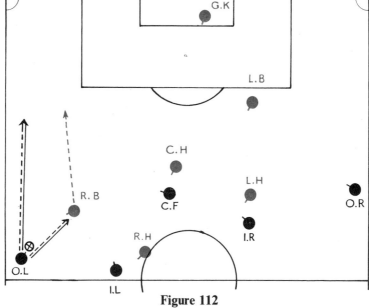

Figure 112

tration of defensive players. In these circumstances, attackers must be prepared to move close to defenders and also to move towards them with the ball, often quickly. We have already seen how screening is an important technique against tightly marking defenders since it can be used to force defenders to make a challenge. In the same way a forward with the ball who is prepared to go straight towards a defender commits him.

In *fig*. 110 the IR in possession moves across the field keeping away from defenders. The opposing IL will shadow him across the field and the rest of the defence behind him will balance accordingly. The IR is not committing the defence or even his immediate opponent in any way.

In *fig*. 111 the IR is moving directly towards the opposing defender (IL) and thus his move will make the IL react in a positive way. Should he fall back or should he make a challenge? The decision is being forced upon him. In the previous situation the IL could afford to wait and see what the developments were likely to be.

In *fig*. 112 where the OL has the ball under control he can move down the line towards the corner-flag. The RB can shadow him and nearby defenders have time to cover and balance accordingly. If the OL however suddenly runs at the RB he is forcing the decision onto the full-back. Other defenders must be prepared for a pass or for the OL beating the RB on either side. They are therefore committed to taking positive action.

TACTICS IN DEFENCE

Organization in defence is easy to achieve provided that players fully understand the principles of the game, and this is true at any level of football. But it is often disturbing to see schoolboy players moving or standing in certain parts of the field, not because play demands it, but because a misguided although no doubt enthusiastic, teacher or coach has told them to. If young players are not capable of understanding their function in a team, tactics and systems must not be imposed upon them. Imitation without understanding is bad.

Defensive play depends basically on players covering each other and, as we have seen, restricting the amount of time and space which is available to opposing attacking players to work in. Using the three areas of the field which can be identified as:

1. Attacking area.
2. Mid-field or build-up area.
3. Defending area.

we can see how different defensive tactics can be applied.

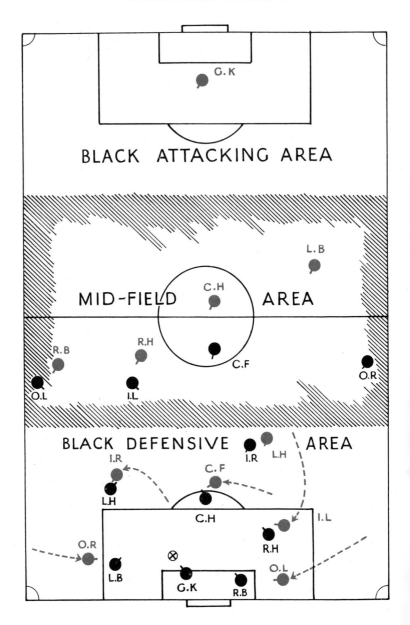

Figure 113

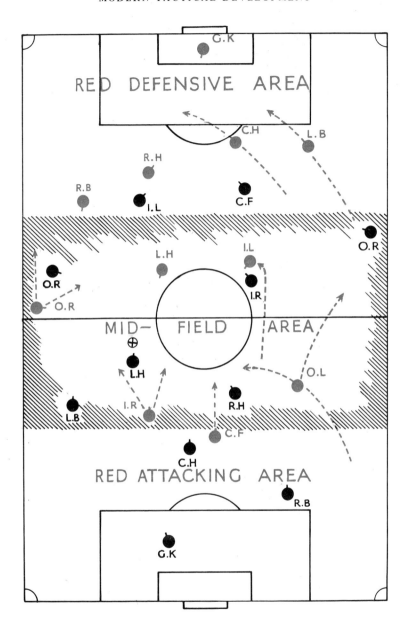

Figure 114

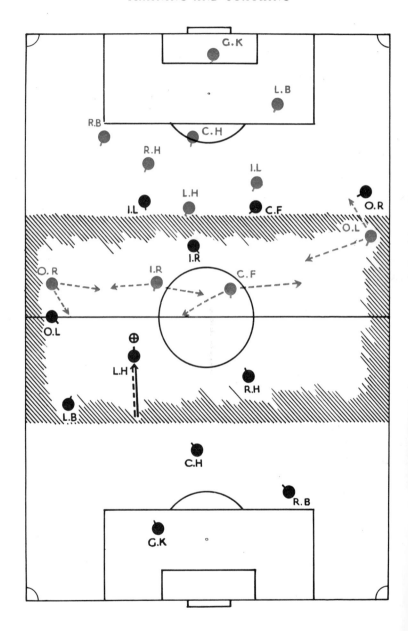

Figure 115

In *fig.* 113 a red attack has broken down in the opponents' penalty-area and the black goalkeeper has the ball. Obviously the red team's tactics must be to regain possession, if possible, in that attacking area. At the very least they must try to make accurate and controlled use of the ball very difficult for the black team. The red forwards will mark the nearest opposing defenders tightly. Black players in mid-field will be covered but not so tightly since the further they are away from goal the greater the time available for the red players to move and to challenge. If the black team is now successful in establishing control of the situation, the opposing forwards will continue to harry them when the ball is near but, at the same time, these forwards will be increasingly conscious of threatening through-passes in the centre of the field. They will not all mark quite so tightly. Mid-field players will think principally of retreating in order to make through-passes difficult.

As the opposing attack moves towards the defending area all the red players who are immediately concerned with defence will fall back to their defensive zones and more advanced players will begin to look for positions in which they may receive the ball when it has been cleared. Reduced to its simplest forms, defence involves:

1. Reducing space.
2. Marking opposing players on a 'man-to-man' basis.

The defensive tactics which we have just studied involve fairly tight man-for-man marking near to the opponents' goal and is known as 'a half field press'. Our aim is to regain possession in our opponents' half of the field and to make it difficult for opposing players to keep possession.

HALF RETREATING DEFENCE

In *fig.* 114 the forwards harass opponents who are near to them and particularly from behind. The main defensive players retreat slowly so as to make a challenge if opportunity occurs but also reduce the possibility of effective through-passes being made.

THE FULL RETREATING DEFENCE

In this method of play ball possession determines defensive policy. As soon as the opposition gain possession of the ball (*fig.* 115) the whole team falls back in front of them to produce a series of defensive barriers. The forward barrier threatens the line of through-passes.

119

4 Reading
the Game

Reading the game is the ability to understand what is happening and, as a consequence, to anticipate immediate or future developments. Some players appear to have a natural capacity for it, while sometimes, even experienced players have only a shallow grasp of it, probably because, in their formative years, they were merely told what to do and not why it should be done. Until a player can read a game he cannot play an authoritative part, in the widest sense, in directing its course. All players should, therefore, strive to develop their ability to read the game.

An analysis of a game must be methodical to be accurate. Here are some of the questions which the experienced observer must ask himself in order to form an objective analysis:

1. Which team is establishing control of the game in terms of:
    (*a*) Territorial advantage?
    (*b*) Ball possession?

2. Is this control the result of:
    (*a*) Tight marking?
    (*b*) Loose marking by opponents?
    (*c*) Physical domination by certain players?
    (*c*) Errors in play of an unforced kind?

These questions, or more particularly the answers to them, begin to locate the sources of weakness or strength.

3. To what extent are the principles of play being ignored or exploited?
    (*a*) Is there depth defensively?

(b) Does an attack show variation?

(c) To what extent does the team which has lost possession over-commit itself to regain possession?

These, and other questions relate to the basic principles of the game, provide answers which are useful in formulating ideas of team play. Players can be singled out for their apparent individual strengths and weaknesses. These may be the result of strengths and deficiencies in other players. For example, a player who gets into reasonable shooting positions himself and then passes may be passing over the final responsibility to a colleague because he, himself, is unwilling to accept the responsibility. If the player to whom the ball is passed misses the goal he looks a bad player when the fault may not be entirely his own.

4. Is a team being stretched territorially? Is this because of:
   (a) Defenders not supporting attacking play closely enough? If so, which defenders?
   (b) Attackers failing to recover to link up with defenders? If so, which attackers?
   (c) Attackers running away from the man with the ball, particularly when he is behind them?
   (d) Defenders retreating too soon and too quickly?

5. What is the work rate of a team and the individual players within it? Football is a game in which it is easy to hide. Some players work hard when the game is going well and fail to work when it goes badly. It is also possible for players to appear to work when, although their energy output is in fact high, they are deliberately working in the wrong place at the wrong time. These are the players who will not expose themselves to the possibility of failure. More responsible players look bad as a consequence.

6. What is a team's tactical pattern?
   (a) Who are the principal feeders?
   (b) Where and how do these feeders gain possession of the ball?
   (c) Who are the principal receivers?
   (d) Where do they move, generally speaking, to receive passes?

7. Is domination coming from team rhythm and effort?
   (a) How can team rhythm be disturbed?

8. Is the dominant team being given too much time or too much space, or both?

121

(*a*) Which players require tight marking?

(*b*) Which players are failing to contain play well?

Some players, when defending, do so loosely in the sense that opponents are allowed too much space in which to manoeuvre. All opposing players, particularly when in possession of the ball, must be contained. This does not necessarily mean they must be tackled, but they must be made to work hard for what they are trying to achieve.

9. Where does a team try to penetrate from?

    (*a*) What methods are used to penetrate near to the penalty-area?

    (*b*) Is penetration attempted late or early?

10. Does a side try to attack from certain areas of the field?

11. What are the strengths and weaknesses of individual players?

There are many other questions which must be asked but for 'game reading' to become accurate it must be logical. Too often our attention is drawn to and focussed upon one aspect of play or one player. This we are able to criticize. Unfortunately, this criticism tends to be destructive since we have not enough information upon which to be constructive.

PART II

Principles of Training and Training Methods

5 Analysis of Playing Requirements

Most of the generalizations made in this chapter refer to the preparation of first-class adult players. The principles stated must be applied at all levels, however, but methods should be adapted to suit the time and facilities available. Below the ages of fifteen or sixteen skill must be the all important factor. In the normal process of growth boys will become stronger provided that they lead vigorously active lives. Strength, power, and endurance will rarely require special consideration. The amount of time which boys devote to vigorous play is decreasing, however, and it is reasonable to expect Physical Education to compensate for this deficiency. As boys mature, consideration of specific fitness increases in importance. During recent years considerable advances in the field of sports physiology have improved the efficiency of training methods. These developments have brought about improved training effects while reducing the amount of time needed to achieve them.

What are the training priorities in terms of the time required by each aspect of player preparation?

1. Team and group skill.
2. Individual technique.
3. Organic fitness.

All coaches realize that the development of highly co-ordinated team play is the most difficult objective. It follows that the greatest proportion of time must be devoted to it. Next in degree of difficulty comes the improvement in the range of individual techniques which each player possesses. Finally we come to organic fitness which, because of the knowledge at our disposal, we can achieve most easily and in a reasonably predictable amount of time.

1. TEAM AND GROUP SKILL

Training usually takes the form of:
- (*a*) Match practice.
- (*b*) Small-sided games.
- (*c*) Functional training: phase practice.
- (*d*) Tactical practice.

Match practice is used to develop systems of play and general tactical awareness. Small-sided games are used to emphasize the principles of play and group tactical possibilities of a general nature. Functional training and phase practice are used to develop the understanding between relatively small groups of players. Tactical practice relates to set plays in various phases of the game.

2. INDIVIDUAL TECHNIQUE

Players are coached in new techniques or attention is given to individual strengths and weaknesses. Practice and coaching situations vary a great deal. Some players may respond to intensive repetitive practice while others may work under fairly closely controlled circumstances. Generally speaking players should be educated to undertake a great deal of the work on their own. The encouragement of players to coach each other has a great deal to offer in this respect, at all levels of the game.

3. ORGANIC FITNESS

Whatever a player may be required to do in training he must be considered as a whole person. He reacts mentally and physically to each and every situation. Certain requirements of training, however, make a specialized consideration necessary. These considerations arise from the development of our knowledge concerning strength, power, and endurance. A soccer player is expected to produce peak performances once or twice a week for eight or nine months. Match conditions vary enormously and the effects of sustained competition are difficult to calculate objectively. Analyses of match demands have been undertaken from time to time and the following conclusions appear to have some validity. These analyses relate to professional players and, therefore, reflect maximum work loads.

	Yards
Total distances covered vary between ...	1,750–6,000
Running at speed	250–2,000
Walking or jogging	1,500–4,000

These figures are comparable to those calculated in similar investigations conducted in Czechoslovakia. Obviously a player's function in a team will affect his work load but the coach will base his fitness programme on the maximum if in any doubt.

The nature of the ·work involved may be broken down as follows:

1. Most all-out or near all-out runs are made without a ball although a ball contact may occur at the beginning or end of such a run.
2. Most of these runs tend to be straight and vary in length between five and fifty yards with the greatest frequency at about thirty yards.
3. A player's movements involve turning quickly, dodging, twisting, weaving, jumping, and leaping and accelerating from stationary or near-stationary positions.
4. Frequently a player is involved in movements where he receives a pass, controls the ball, and makes another pass.
5. Many of the player's movements must be made while anticipating a challenge from an opponent.

The qualities of fitness involved are:
1. Endurance—both local and general.
2. Power.
3. Speed and agility.
4. Flexibility.

Where some of these qualities can be developed in one and the same activity and involving movement patterns from the game, both with and without a ball, so much the better. Care must be taken, however, since it is easy for a coach to be deluded into thinking that a vigorous and interesting activity (from the players' point of view) is achieving all the fitness objectives. During work in which skill is the main objective it is probable that physiological adaptation in terms of the development of power or endurance, for example, will be of an insignificant order. Where a player is required to work hard over a relatively short period of time in order to improve cardiac (heart) efficiency, for example, activities which require skill in their execution will probably reduce the efficiency of the activity so far as physiological adaptation is concerned.

6 Endurance and Speed

Endurance may be defined as the ability to take part in moderately intensive activity for a prolonged period. Intensive activity may take place during this period but the nature of the activity will permit compensating periods of partial recovery. Here a player works for two periods of forty-five minutes with fairly long periods of moderate activity interspersed with short periods of highly intensive activity.

There are obviously two kinds of endurance. In the first total bodily effort takes place over a long period at various intensities and continues until fatigue becomes evident: movements become laboured and unco-ordinated. The player can be seen to be forcing himself into continued activity and he is obviously distressed. In soccer the onset of fatigue is most apparent in the deterioration of skill, and those skills in which the player is weakest will deteriorate first and most rapidly. Clearer evidence of fatigue can be seen when the game is played in severe climatic conditions or when ground conditions are extremely difficult. A continuation of fatigue results in collapse from exhaustion. Where this occurs in football it is usually in conditions of extreme cold or heat: the system through which fuel is made available for effort breaks down temporarily.

The endurance which is required to sustain total body effort for long periods is circulo-respiratory endurance. Let us look at the physiological nature of circulo-respiratory endurance as it affects the soccer player.

The movement which takes place at any joint is the result of muscular contraction. This is just as true of the movement of the eye-lids in blinking as it is of the knee joint in running and walking.

127

Almost every movement we make and almost every position the human body can adopt is caused or held by muscular contraction. The fuel which is used during muscular contraction is oxygen and, of course, the transporter of oxygen is blood. As oxygen is used so the blood must be re-oxygenized and this is achieved through the respiratory system. This involves the intake and output of air and the organs through which oxygen is taken from the air and into the blood. In simple terms, the respiratory system consists of the air intake and exhaust channels together with the lungs, which are the organs concerned with the transfer of oxygen from the air to the blood stream.

The circulatory system transports blood to the various parts of the body where it is to be used. The same system also transports the blood away from the centre of activity where oxygen has been used and where the chemical changes involved in active tissue have caused the oxygen to be returned with the waste products of this process in the form of carbon dioxide (CO_2). The blood returns again, passing through the lung system and is re-oxygenated, hence the use of the term circulation or circulatory system.

The more vigorous an activity the greater will be the frequency of muscular contraction. The more frequent the muscular contraction, the greater the demand for oxygen will be. This means that some form of pumping mechanism is needed to effect a supply of blood to and from the various parts of the body. The heart is just such a pumping mechanism. It becomes obvious, therefore, that the harder the muscles work, the harder the heart must work to supply blood (and therefore oxygen) and consequently the faster the intake of air (i.e. the quicker the breathing) to supply oxygen to the blood stream through the lungs. The signs of intense effort as anyone can see or feel are:

1. Hardening of muscle, showing contraction.
2. Increase in heart beat or pulse rate, as it is known.
3. Increased rate of breathing.

If intensive activity is undertaken regularly we can see physical changes taking place. Muscles become firmer, more clearly defined against the skin and, to a certain extent, bigger. The heart, being a muscle in exactly the same way, is also subjected to the same changes; it becomes bigger and stronger in order to cope with the increased demand for blood which bigger and stronger muscles will make. But whatever increase in muscle strength or endurance is achieved through training, it is just as quickly lost when the intensity of activity drops. The body, and all its parts, including the heart, is constantly adjusting to the nature of the demands which are made upon it, in other words, fitness for work is quickly adjusted to suit the nature of the work. One of the consequences of age is that the body loses the capacity to adapt quickly and one of the characteristics of youth is that the process of growth is an anticipation of the demands which may be made upon the body in adulthood. Growing children will grow stronger naturally, but if they are to become well-grown, they need years of vigorously active play in order that the growth process should be stimulated to its maximum potential. The later we leave this the greater will be the difficulties to overcome.

The second kind of endurance is the ability of a muscle or muscle group to be active in a moderately intensive way for a sustained period of time. This is the endurance missing when a player, although apparently generally fit and unfatigued, suffers from cramp. In the soccer player cramp may be located in the muscles behind the bones of the lower leg, responsible for raising the body on the toes, as in sprinting. The ability to repeat muscular actions for a long period of time where one muscle or a localized group of muscles are exercised is known as localized endurance. Obviously, circulo-respiratory and localized muscular endurance are closely related. When a muscle or localized muscle-group is working, contraction is followed by relaxation. Contraction causes a shortening of the muscle, or an attempted shortening, and blood is squeezed out into the veins which are the blood-returning channels of the circulatory system. As the muscle relaxes so blood is drawn back into muscle and a chemical exchange occurs which allows further contractions or work to take place. It is likely that prolonged and rapid sequences of contraction and relaxation, where the load may be high, produce a condition in which the waste products of exercise are inefficiently dealt with. This inefficiency stimulates, through the nervous system, some form of cut-out mechanism whereby the muscle is no longer able to respond to its requirements. This may take the form of an inability to produce a contraction of sufficient intensity to do the required work or the muscle may go into spasm and produce cramp pains. Cramps and fatigue are not necessarily the same thing but both or either may indicate circulatory inefficiency or lack of local endurance.

According to Egolinskii, a Russian researcher working in this field, the development of endurance is determined by the following factors:

1. The size of the load on the muscles during training.
2. The rate of exercise.
3. The duration of exercise.

4. The rate of the activity.
5. The interval between bouts of activity.
6. The length of the training period.
7. The level of pre-training endurance.
8. Individual differences (which might involve temperament, physical type, etc.).

Of these the load on the muscles and the rate of the exercise are the most important. Morehouse and Rasch, American research workers, state that 'repeated performance in a sporting event, whatever its nature, will produce a large measure of improvement of endurance for that event', in other words, endurance fitness is specific, to a great extent, to the particular activity for which endurance training is undertaken.

There is no doubt that, so far as over-all improvement in any activity requiring skill is concerned, practice of that skill situation and coaching in it will produce improvement. However, repeated practice of a skill is not enough to bring an athlete or player to the peak of endurance.

Is there any evidence which will help us in determining training loads and intensities so far as endurance is concerned? Professor A. V. Hill's work on the physiology of exercise has been the basis of what is known as 'steady state' training. This type of training involves the player in near all out efforts for an extended period of time. In this way the player is trained to develop a tolerance towards the chemical effects of sustained intense activity. It has been calculated that all-out effort in conditions where oxygen is not readily available produces blood lactates at the rate of three grammes per second. When there is a concentration of 130 grammes of lactic acid in the blood the human organism collapses. This means that approximately forty-five seconds of such work will produce collapse. Training for soccer should be of such a nature that the player should always be able to continue activity, therefore all out efforts are not required for this period of time.

Endurance training must prepare the player for the severe and varying demands which the game will make upon him. For certain brief periods of time the effort made by a player will be performed in near anaerobic conditions. These are conditions in which muscular contractions are required but where the availability of oxygen is slight or non-existent. Obviously the more efficient the body is to become in working under these conditions the more the tolerance towards such conditions must be increased. In other words, the player must experience the stress of anaerobic work in such a way as to assist him to cope with such stresses in the game.

Since we know that forty-five seconds, approximately, is the longest time during which all-out effort can be sustained should we concentrate on runs of that duration? The answer lies in the circumstances of competition. The soccer players needs to be able to withstand stress over a long period of time. The inducement of a state of collapse will prevent further work from taking place and the resulting adaptation will not relate to what is required for the game. The basis of training work for cardio-respiratory fitness is now taking shape.

1. The duration of each training sprint will not be greater than thirty-forty seconds.
2. The improvement in adaptation will be achieved by:
   (a) increasing the number of training stints and maintaining the recovery periods constant,
   (b) decreasing the length of the recovery periods,
   (c) a combination of both.

The maximum distance to be aimed at will be something of the order of 2,000 yards. The remaining distance of 4,000 yards, which takes the form of light work (i.e. jogging or walking) should be more than adequately covered during general skill training.

We can now establish endurance and speed training principles as follows:

1. Players should be trained to endure a maximum of 2,000 yards *intensive* running activity.
2. Sprint distances should be over a maximum of fifty yards or for a maximum of forty seconds and should involve movement patterns from the game.
3. Players should experience playing the game, when feeling stress, in practice circumstances.
4. Since skill can seriously interfere with the intensity of training effort, some boosting of endurance training is necessary. This will be best achieved outside game or skill considerations.

The bulk of training where cardio-respiratory fitness is the objective will be devoted to the following methods:

1. Repetition maze runs.
2. Pressure training.
3. Skill drill repetition runs.
4. Interval running with or without skill requirements.
5. Circuit training.

The variety of activity is necessary since the simple answer to endurance is hard, intensive work. Work of this nature must be demanding and yet interesting and such a pill is difficult to swallow whatever the coating which may be added and, of course, the more one tries to add coating the less effective the pill becomes.

Fortunately we have these five possibilities at our disposal for maintaining and increasing training loads, and they are to a certain extent measurable and progressive. In this way the trainer can devise blocks of work probably of a month's duration with two different methods employed together giving variety. Similarly, over a season different combinations of endurance training methods will increase this variety and thus maintain maximum interest. Players must be afforded every opportunity to understand what we are trying to do and this can be achieved by encouraging all the players to become active in recording and checking the work and recovery rates achieved. In this way they become familiar with their own performances. This is vital in any training programme. We cannot expect players to submit blindly and without intelligence to training; they must be actively engaged not only physically but also mentally.

REPETITION MAZE RUNS

The maze run is an attempt to simulate the running patterns of players in the game and, at the same time, to produce controlled training loads and intensities. Here are some suggested preparations for laying on a maze run:

1. Each player is timed for his fastest time, over the course once.
2. If individual times are less than thirty seconds then the course is too easy and additional obstacles should be put in.
3. According to the players' state of training, teams may be as many as six in number or as low as two and will work in relays. This means that for a team of six, each player will perform one interval of work and then have five intervals of rest while his team mates are running their work intervals. As the players become accustomed to the work the number in each team should be reduced to two, three or four. This means that one work interval is now followed by one, two, or three rest intervals. While this adjustment to training is taking place, the number of repetitions remains the same. The ultimate number of repetitions will be the equivalent of 2,000 yards, that is to say, when working over a 50-80-yard course, something in the order of thirty-forty repetitions. Each group of five will be competing against each other and the composition of the teams should be evenly balanced so far as individual players' speeds are concerned.

132

Using each player's all-out test time, spot checks can be made upon the extent to which individuals are working hard. When the groups have been reduced to three or four the process of stepping up the total number of repetitions can begin. A starting distance of 800 yards or ten repetitions will be suitable for most players if they are in a low state of training. Because of its competitive nature, interest in this sort of activity is retained for an extended period. Assuming that these runs are used twice a week, the course can be stepped up by five repetitions (250 yards) each week for six weeks, or more rapidly depending upon the training response of the players. Teams should be given their total course time and indeed target times can be established based upon their single repetition test times. Records of performance must be kept and displayed as an incentive. It should be said here that the race distance (e.g. ten reps. or 800 yards, etc.) is covered by *each* member of the group. A running maze can be used equally effectively indoors or out depending upon the equipment available.

In *fig.* 116 the total distance covered will be approximately 80-110 yards. Obstacle (a) is a vaulting box or any firm obstacle at a height of about four feet. Players must touch down on the box with at least one foot in going over it. Obstacle (b) consists of four hurdles about two yards apart, the first of which is no more than five yards from the box. This prevents players hurdling and forces them to jump. Obstacle (c) consists of a series of poles or chairs a yard apart. The player weaves in and out without touching them. A circle is marked on the ground one yard from the last pole and it should be five-seven yards from the end of the course which can also be marked by a circle. The player makes four shuttle or return

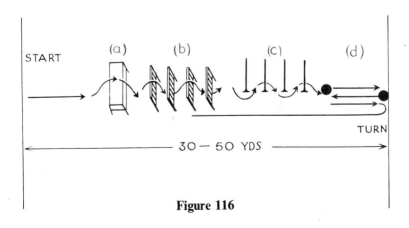

Figure 116

trips here and he must touch the inside of each circle on each trip. The course finishes with a straight run back to the starting line.

As previously explained the work is carried out on a relay basis. The number in each team determines the number of rest intervals to each work interval. Obviously for each team there must be another course.

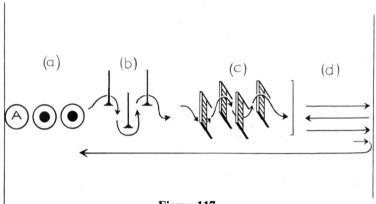

Figure 117

In *fig.* 117 the first 'obstacle' consists of footballs in circles which are five yards from the starting line and five yards apart. The first player brings the balls back to (a) one at a time. He then weaves in and out of the poles at (b). The hurdle obstacles at (c) are alternately 2 ft. 6 in. and 3 ft. 6 in. high. The player goes under the low hurdles and over the high ones and, again, they are two yards apart. The final 'obstacle' at (d) is again a series of shuttle runs.

PRESSURE TRAINING

Pressure training involves submitting a player to a controlled repetition of ball service where he is required to produce one or two soccer techniques on receiving the ball. As the player under pressure becomes accustomed to the practice, so the rate of ball service is increased. *Fig.* 118 illustrates a simple form of pressure training practice. Player X^6 stands in the centre of a circle of five other players, each of the five players having a ball. Beginning with player X^1, and proceeding clockwise, a high ball is served to X^6 who might be required to control the ball in a specific way (e.g. chest trap) and give a return push-pass to the server. According to the proficiency of X^6 so the next service is delivered earlier or later.

Pressure is exerted on X^6 by virtue of the fact that he can never take much time over dealing with any service; the next server will determine how much time X^6 has.

When technique begins to show signs of deteriorating, X^6 leaves the centre and changes place with one of the players in the circle. This sort of practice was used to intensify practice in the

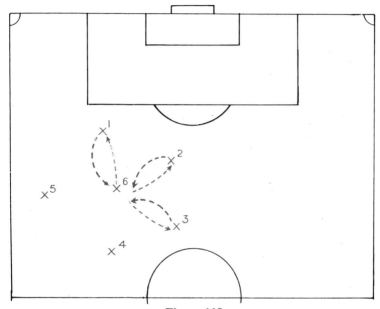

Figure 118

belief that such a degree of repetitive practice at speed would help the player to develop the technique in such a way as to make it a part of his playing techniques. This belief may be open to serious doubts. However, it quickly became apparent that, with minor adaptations, a player could be made to work extremely hard in pressure training. It is recommended that where pressure training is used it should be undertaken with one serious aim in mind. It is likely that this work is more useful in causing an improvement in general and local endurance than it is in bringing about an improvement in skill.

In organizing pressure practices where the objective is heart-lung and heart-muscle fitness, the following points should be remembered.

135

1. The quality of technique is not as important as the intensity of work.
2. The player must be involved in intensive running or jumping over reasonable distances. If the area used is small and, therefore, the distances covered are also small, the effect of the work will begin to emphasize local endurance rather than general endurance. In other words, his legs are likely to give up before the required demands can be made upon his heart and lungs.
3. The greater the number of players involved, the greater will be the number of rest intervals and thus the less effective the training will become. Obviously complicated practice organization is not recommended.
4. The overall aim is still to produce intensive work periods each of which will be thirty-forty seconds in duration, which can be sustained over an increasing number of repetitions with decreasing rest intervals.

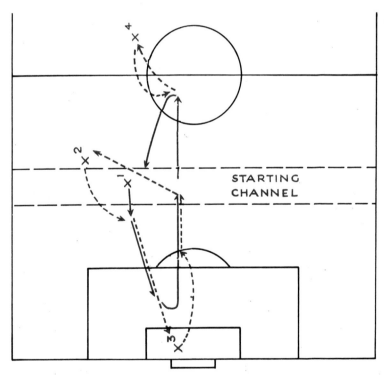

STARTING
CHANNEL

Figure 119

In *fig.* 119 X^1 is the working man of a four-man team. The pattern of service and movement is as follows: X^1 standing in the channel marked by dotted lines receives a lobbed service from X^2. He controls the ball, takes it beyond the penalty-spot and shoots. X^3 is not a goalkeeper, merely a server who then serves a ball to drop in the penalty-area restraining arc. X^1 turns, controls the ball and takes it into the starting channel and pushes a short pass to X^2.

Continuing his run, he receives a service from X^4, waiting in the centre circle, and heads the ball back to X^4. X^1 then returns to the starting channel. Depending upon the size of the pitch, the total distance covered by X^1 on one complete trip will be sixty-ninety yards. We now need a rough guide as to the number of trips which should make up one work stint. We must use our quickest players to find out how many trips produce a work stint of about

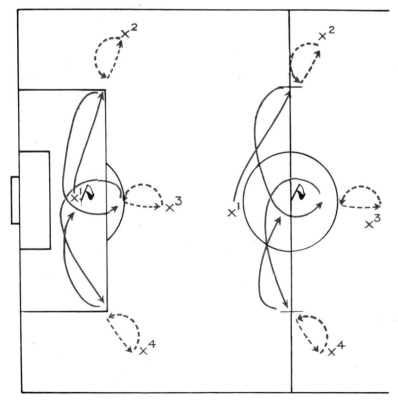

Figure 120

thirty seconds. The slower players will take longer which ensures that all the players are working for the required amount of time.

At the end of each work stint the players can change round. The worker, in the example, X^1, runs to the goalmouth. X^3 runs to the centre circle. X^4 takes over at X^2 and X^2 becomes the worker. Obviously other teams can work using the same boundary lines and thus the session can be based upon team competition. It is probable that with adult players, three trips will be made in thirty-forty seconds by each player or a total of 170-250 yards. The competition can be based upon a set number of work turns for each individual player.

In *fig.* 120 the same principle is applied. Here we are using the width of the penalty-area together with a ten-yard radius which is provided by the centre-circle and the penalty-area restraining arc as our distance markers. Starting on the penalty-spot X^1 runs to receive a service which is aimed to drop on the corner of the penalty-area. He gives a first-time pass back to X^2. X^1 then turns and runs back around the flag on the penalty-spot and turns to receive a service from X^3, which is aimed to drop on the edge of the restraining arc. He plays the ball, after controlling it, back to X^3. Turning once again around the flag, he then runs to receive the ball from X^4. A full trip here will be approximately 100 yards and, again, the required number of trips will be calculated as in *fig.* 119. *Fig.* 120 also shows how another team can work using the centre circle.

Fig. 121 shows a similar pattern. X^1 runs to receive a service from X^4 controlling it inside the restraining arc; he turns and takes the ball to the goal area. He can only shoot from inside the area. X^2 is a retriever responsible for supplying balls to X^3 and X^4. After shooting, X^1 turns and collects a service from X^3. He takes the ball inside the restraining arc and pushes a short pass to X^4. The trip is then repeated. $O^{1\ 4}$ shows how another team can work at the same time.

Each trip will be approximately forty yards and, therefore, it may be necessary to have four or five trips in a work stint. After each stint the players move anti-clockwise. X^1 goes to X^4, X^4 moves to X^3, X^3 moves to X^2 and X^2 becomes the working player.

There are many possible variations and all will be effective provided that the principles of training are applied.

REPETITION SKILL DRILLS

Skill drills can be used to develop heart and lung, or cardio-respiratory fitness. These are almost exclusively for outdoor use

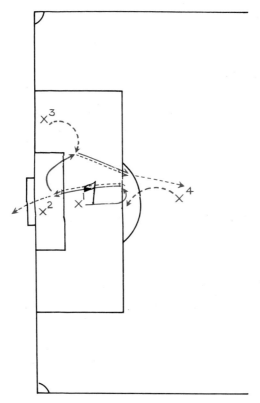

Figure 121

since the size of the area required is at least the equivalent of a soccer pitch. Once again, however, the more complicated the drill pattern becomes the less effective the work will be. The accent must be upon sustained high-speed work.

The first example (*fig.* 122) is a simple shuttle relay in which players are working for one stint and resting for three. For players in a reasonable state of training this should be within their capabilities. The rest interval can be reduced to two stints using only

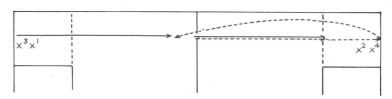

Figure 122

three players to a team and the relay must always start at the end which begins with two players. In the example given there is a ball at each end. X^2 kicks the ball into the opposing half of the field and as soon as the ball has been kicked X^1 can move forward to collect and control it. X^1 then runs with the ball into the zone made by the penalty-area and an extension of it. When he moves into this zone he can pass to X^4. As soon as X^4 receives the ball behind the goal line, he holds it up, which is the signal for X^3 to kick the other ball downfield. X^2 moves forward and this drill is repeated a set number of times if a team contest is used. This is an excellent form of interval training for a large number of players. The players are covering sixty-five to ninety-five yards at speed depending upon the size of the pitch. The maximum number of repetitions to build up to in the unit of time during which this form of training is used is between twenty and thirty according to whether the pitch is 130 yards or 100 yards in length.

In *fig.* 123 the players are working in teams of nine made up of three squads of three players. As in the previous example, the work stint consists of one length of the pitch. The relay will start at the end which has two squads. The interpassing drill used is illustrated in *fig.* 123. The centre man (X^1) pushes the ball in front of X^2 and runs outside and past him (stage a). X^2, who is now the centre man, pushes the ball in front of X^3 and runs outside and past him (stage b). The drill is repeated until the whole squad has entered the penalty-area zone (stage c). The ball may then be released to the next squad. It is important that the ball is pushed well in front of the receiving player in order that high speed can be maintained. Accuracy is not vitally important since we are aiming at effort rather than skill. If this work stint is too short, the following variation may Se used. All three squads start at the same end of the pitch and each work stint consists of two lengths of the field.

Using a four-man squad the drill pattern might be as in *fig.* 124. X^1 plays the ball diagonally in front of X^3 and runs past X^4. X^3 plays the ball back to X^2. X^2 plays the ball diagonally in front of X^1 and runs past X^3. The drill is repeated in the same way throughout. Here the drill is more complicated and, therefore, all teams should work over two lengths of the field on each stint.

Repetition running can be used indoors in a gymnasium or hall of any size in the following way, provided that rebound surfaces in the form of blank walls or gymnasium benches are available. The teams are placed behind the benches or at a suitable point along the walls of the gymnasium (*fig.* 125). Once again the size of each team is determined by the players' state of training and the severity of work required from them. Working anti-clockwise

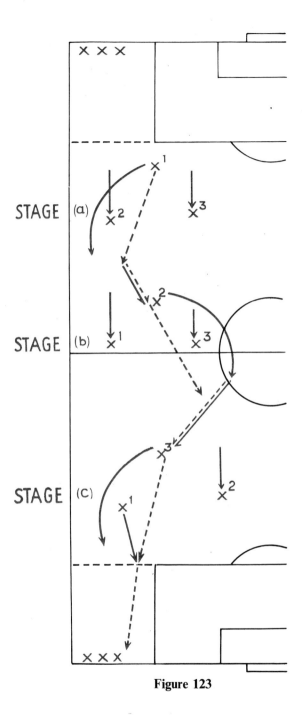

Figure 123

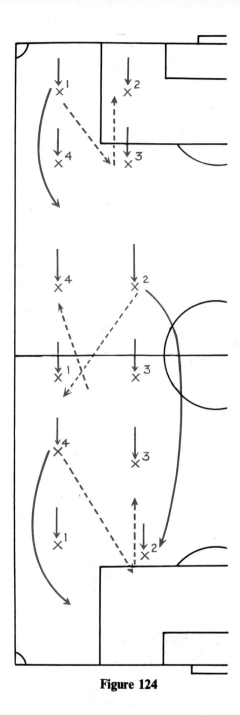

Figure 124

(*fig.* 125), the first man in each team begins by playing a wall pass off each of the rebound points at PQRSTU. He starts at the point which is next to his own in an anti-clockwise direction and finishes with a pass onto his own rebound point. The teams work as relay teams. In a normal gymnasium it is recommended that the work stint shall be two circuits which will mean a distance of approxi-

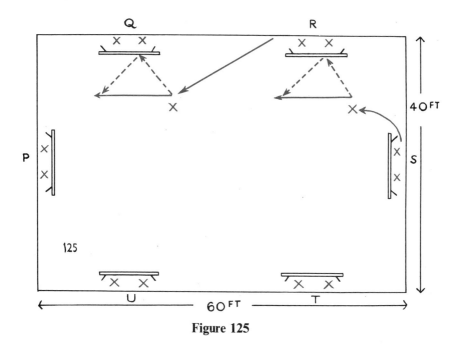

Figure 125

mately 100 yards. In bigger halls the distance should be calculated in terms of the time taken to complete one or more circuits. We are still aiming at a work stint of maximum all out effort which lasts between thirty and forty seconds. The total distance covered will be again built up progressively to 2,000 yards.

7 Strength and Power

Strength can be defined as the ability to overcome a resistance without the assistance of speed or momentum of any kind. Power is the result of applied strength: the ability to move a resistance at speed. Obviously, the greater the speed at which the resistance is moved the more powerful the performer. The soccer player is, therefore, only concerned with the development of strength in so far as it makes him more powerful in those aspects of performance which require power. Thus the resistance with which the player is concerned are:

1. His own body weight.
2. The ball.
3. The varying resistances produced by different ground and climatic conditions.

Examples of the circumstances in which a player exerts power against the above resistances are as follows:

1. When jumping to head the ball or to save in the case of a goalkeeper.
2. When running quickly, particularly from a standing or near stationary start.
3. When changing direction or turning.
4. When kicking the ball powerfully (i.e. shooting for goal).
5. When playing on heavy grounds or against strong winds.

As with all physiological changes which are brought about by training, strength and, therefore, power can only be increased by subjecting the body to stress. In the case of strength and power training the stress is produced by increasing the resistance against which a muscle or group of muscles are required to contract. The muscle or group of muscles are subjected to 'overload'. Obviously the resistance provided by a player's body weight and by the ball remain relatively constant and, therefore, power training must involve additional or external resistances of some kind. There are two basic methods of strength training, isometric and isotonic.

The first involves muscle contraction without any shortening of the muscle fibres being possible, as for example when a person tries to push down a wall or some other immovable object. The second involves the contraction of muscle with actual shortening of the muscle fibres, such as when a man pushes a heavy movable object.

It is argued that a player need only be concerned with the power necessary to move his own body and the ball effectively. But how do we measure effect? In a competitive sport effect is measured against other players' capabilities. In other words each player must develop his capabilities to the highest possible functional level. He must be able to run, to jump, to turn, and to shoot as hard and as fast as he can.

The most effective form of isotonic training is with weights. Many people in sport confuse weight-training with weight-lifting which is, of course, a competitive application of weight-training. A further misconception is that training with weights is time-consuming; in fact the opposite is true. If a training system is efficient it achieves the required effect in the shortest possible time and our aim in football is to devote the maximum time available to skill. This being so, physiological adaptation must be achieved quickly.

The basic principles of weight training are as follows: the lighter the weight used the more the player is affecting local endurance. For power, therefore, we need fairly heavy weights to provide an effective resistance. It has been found that the number of repetitions of an exercise designed to improve power must be not more than ten. The standard by which a player's capabilities can be determined is whether or not he can perform the repetitions maintaining good form. If he tries to adopt abnormal trunk and limb positions during the exercise and where he shows he is having to 'fight' the weight, he is using too heavy a weight.

The player should then practice the exercises in his schedule with a very light weight, perhaps only a bar without the plates. This will usually mean that he is only handling 15 lbs. The aim is to ensure that he is familiar with the most effective and, therefore, the safest way of handling a weight. The technique of handling weights is referred to in the section on circuit training on pages 151-153.

During the familiarization period, which may take three weeks with two or three sessions each week, the poundages can be gradually increased while experimenting with different numbers of repetitions. When a poundage has been reached where less than ten repetitions can be performed without a rest and while maintaining good style, the player's training schedule can be established.

Exercises which are suitable for the development of power as it is applied in soccer are as follows:

1. *Vertical jumps* (*plate* 1). The bar is lifted to the thighs using the technique previously referred to. It is raised to the chest and then

Plate 1   **Plate 2**

lifted over the head and rested across the player's shoulders behind the neck. The player bends his knees until his thighs are almost at right-angles to his shins. From this position he leaps upwards as powerfully as he can returning to land on his toes with bent knees to absorb the shock of landing.

2. *Split squats* (*plate* 2). The bar is lifted to the chest as in the previous exercise. The player then adopts a wide split position. He lowers his body by bending both legs until the knee of the forward leg is in front of his foot. The erect position is resumed by a vigorous straightening movement of the front knee. In a schedule, the player should have each leg alternately in the forward position.

3. *Hack lift* (*plates* 3a and 3b). Here the player takes up a position with the barbell behind him. The principles of lifting however are the same. In this exercise it may be necessary to have the heels raised slightly by placing them on wooden blocks or two weight plates approximately one inch high. This prevents the barbell causing the lifter to overbalance backwards. During the lift the player must lean slightly forward from the hips to compensate for the backward pull of the weight.

4. *Heave press with dumbbells or barbell* (*plates* 4a, b, c, and d). The weight is raised to the thighs and then to the chest. The body is dipped slightly by bending the knees. The knees are then straightened vigorously and, at the same time, the barbell is pressed overhead.

5. *Sit ups* (plates 5 and 6). The player lies on his back with his ankles under some firm object or held down by a partner. The weight is held behind the neck. The player then sits up until his trunk is upright.

Plate 3a

Plate 3b

Plate 4a

Plate 4b

Plate 4c

Plate 4d

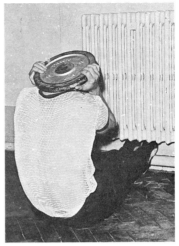

Plate 5   **Plate 6**

6. *Trunk forward bend* (plate 7). The barbell is raised to the thigh, the chest and then placed behind the neck in the shoulder rest position. The upper body is then bent forward from the hips, keeping the head up and the back flat, until it is horizontal to the ground.

Plate 7

During the pre-season period the player would take three of these exercises on one training day and the other three on a second training day, as follows:

Tuesday   (a) Vertical Jumps.
          (b) Sit Ups with Barbell.
          (c) Heave Press with Barbell.
Thursday (a) Split Squats.
          (b) Trunk Forward Bend.
          (c) Hack Lift.

Having warmed up with a few minutes' general exercise, as for any period of competition or training, the player begins his schedule. In the early stages this might be:

Five repetitions of the exercise performed three times with a rest in between each group of five. A number of exercise repetitions performed without a break is known as a set. So that the player does three sets of five repetitions. (This may be shown as 3S × 5R).

When the competitive season begins the player will continue with two weekly sessions but he will reduce the exercises on each occasion to two. These can be:

Tuesday: Either Exercises 1, 2, 3 or 4. Let us say 1 for example.
          And Exercises 5 or 6. Let us say 5 for example.
Thursday: Either Exercises 2, 3 or 4. Let us say 2 for example.
          or Exercise 6.

Working progressively on the exercises selected the player or coach may decide on the following programme for a month or six weeks.

As the player begins to find 3S × 5R easy another set of five repetitions is added until towards the end of the four- or six-week period he is using 5S × 5R on each exercise. The combination of exercises might then be changed.

His new programme can be:

Tuesday: Exercise 3 - 3S × 5R.
          Exercise 6 - 5S × 5R.
Thursday: Exercise 4 - 3S × 5R.
          Exercise 5 - 5S × 5R.

He has used exercises 1 and 2 in the first block of training and this leaves 3 and 4 to be used in the present block. The load is 3S × 5R. Exercises 5 and 6 he has already used and taken to the 5S × 5R level so that he can continue with this level perhaps slightly increasing the poundage.

The reason for dividing the exercises into two groups (i.e. 1, 2, 3 and 4 and 5 and 6) is that the first four exercises are all predominately hip and leg exercises. Exercise 5 is an exercise designed to

150

produce a power increase in the hip flexors and abdominals and exercise 6 is principally a lower back and hip exercise.

The time taken over weight training need not be greater than fifteen to twenty minutes on each weight-training day. The benefits will be considerable over the playing season. Many believe that weight-training produces muscle bulk and, therefore, makes a person stiff, slow, and muscle bound. Research has completely disproved these contentions. Power training with fairly heavy weights makes a player faster, more supple, and certainly more powerful. Training with light weights, where a great number of repetitions are possible, is likely to increase muscle bulk and certainly does not increase power to any great degree. This is not recommended for soccer players.

Weight training is not intended to take the place of skill training; it is intended to supplement it. There are certain physiological changes which cannot take place through ball practice, weight training can make up some of these deficiencies.

CIRCUIT TRAINING

This form of training, as devised by R. Morgan and G. T. Adamson of Leeds University, is intended to provide an intensive training process which can be easily adapted to an individual's requirements. At the same time the system lends itself to controlled progression, an important aspect of any training procedure. Circuit training aims at improving the cardio-respiratory and cardio-vascular functions through increasing repetitions, and to a certain extent loads, and decreasing the total exercise time. Training targets are easily established and, therefore, training effect can be measured.

Exercises can be grouped in the following approximate anatomical divisions:

1. Leg and hip.
2. Arm and shoulder.
3. Trunk in flexion.
4. Trunk in extension.
5. General (where large body movements are involved).

There are basically two kinds of circuits: those requiring apparatus, and those requiring no apparatus. Specialist athletes like the first category since they must train to a higher level than the average.

Most circuits involve eight to twelve exercises and they are arranged so that no two consecutive exercises have the same anatomical effect. Circuit training modified for soccer will have an exercise bias towards: legs and hips, abdominals (trunk in flexion), and general exercises.

Where weights are used the following points of lifting and lowering techniques must be carefully observed (*plates* 4a, b, c and d):

1. Stand as near to the weight as possible.
2. Stoop by lowering the hips and not the back.
3. Feet should be shoulder-width apart.
4. Hands, when grasping a barbell, slightly more than shoulder-width apart.
5. The head is up and the back flat.
6. Basic lifting is achieved by using the legs and hips, not by using the back.

When lowering a weight the above procedure is reversed. Keep the weight close to the body all the time.

The following exercises may be used under each of the five categories:

1. Legs
    (a) Half squats or half-squat jumps.
    (b) Step-ups.
    (c) Hack lift.
2. Trunk in flexion
    (a) Inclined sit-ups.
    (b) Inclined or hanging curls.
    (c) Curls.
3. Trunk in extension
    (a) Bent forward rowing.
    (b) Crab bends.
4. Arm and shoulder
    (a) High press-ups.
    (b) Two-hand press.
5. General
    (a) Rope climbing.
    (b) Hurdle run (over and under).
    (c) Alternate hopping.

In a space 30 ft. by 15 ft., twelve players can be accommodated with ease and it should be possible for eighteen to work without great hindrance to each other.

A balanced circuit for footballers might be:

Exercise	Anatomical Effect	Category
1. Trunk Curls.	Abdominal.	Light.

152

Exercise	Anatomical Effect	Category
2. Half Squat Jumps.	Legs and Hips.	Strong (+ barbell).
3. Back Lifts.	Back.	Light.
4. Box Jump.	General.	Fairly Strong.
5. High Press Ups.	Arm and Shoulder.	Fairly Strong.
6. Hack Lifts.	Legs and Hips.	Strong (+ barbell).
7. Sit Ups.	Abdominals and Hips.	Light.
8. Overhead Press.	Arm and Shoulder.	Strong (+ barbell).
9. Step Ups.	Legs and Hips.	Fairly Strong.
10. Crab Bends.	Back.	Strong.
11. Hurdle Run.	General.	Fairly Strong.

ESTABLISHING TRAINING LOADS AND RATES

1. Players are in pairs, one pair to each exercise position.
2. Each exercise is demonstrated.
3. Players practice each exercise in turn by moving round the circuit. This practice is for technique only.
4. Having practiced, one player works while the other counts and records the score.
5. On exercises 1, 2, 3, 4, 6, 7, 9, and 11 each player performs as many repetitions of the exercise as he can in sixty seconds.
6. On exercises 5, 8, and 10 each player does as many repetitions as he can without a rest.
7. The training load is half his maximum number of repetitions for each exercise.
8. Each player goes once round the circuit using his own training load for each exercise as fast as he can.
9. Double this test time will be his initial target time since when training he will be required to complete two circuits.
10. If the players train in pairs one will work while the other will check his technique on the exercises and generally urge him on. He will also record his partner's time.

As the players' circuit times improve so new and lower target times can be established. Further progression is achieved by periodically re-testing and establishing new training loads and times. A large clock with a sweep second-hand is a useful timepiece. Alternatively an ordinary kitchen timing clock will be satisfactory. Modifications of circuit training which try to avoid the necessity for testing and timing are not satisfactory. Progression is the most important aim and training targets must be controlled if specialized athletes are to gain the maximum benefit from the activity.

153

8 Planned Training and Coaching

Planning a training and coaching programme is vital to the development of top-class performance of any kind. It ensures progression, it enables players to assess their own performances objectively, and at the same time they are able to understand why training and coaching are necessary for the improvement of team performance. The coach who plans his programme is continually forced to think about what he is doing. Without planning he is merely drawing upon his own experience without thinking progressively or analytically. Sooner or later a coach who works in this way finds that he has lost purpose and sooner or later his players realize that the training and coaching has no purpose.

All players are individuals in the widest sense of the word and training and coaching must recognize the need for them to be treated as individuals so far as is humanly possible. All players have easily recognized physiological, psychological, and anatomical differences, and mass training and coaching therefore can have little part to play in their preparation. Interesting changes have taken place and are still taking place in the structure of the football season in England. Until recent years the football year, for the vast majority of players, was as follows: mid-July to mid-August (4-5 weeks)—pre-season training; mid-August to early May (34-35 weeks)—playing season; early May to mid-July (12-14 weeks)—close season.

During recent years we have seen an increase in the close season tours undertaken by leading clubs not only at the end of our season but also before the following season starts. This has resulted in the close season being reduced from sixteen weeks to perhaps six to eight weeks in some cases. The close season referred to here is that period when no competitive football is played in England. Whatever the reason for this contraction of the close season, it results in a reduction of the time during which a player can become totally unfit. Most coaches are fully aware of the serious decline in general and specific fitness which occurs during this period. It is argued that an eight- or nine-month season requires a long lay off to compensate for the psychological and physiological demands which are imposed upon a player. This is true but it is extremely doubtful if players need a break of four months. Indeed the disadvantages of physiological deterioration are not offset by the advantage of psychological relaxation. The extent of this deterioration can be observed in a slower recovery after vigorous activity (as measured by post exercise pulse rate recovery to normal) or in the player's ability to undertake a given amount of work which involves stress on the cardio-respiratory-vascular functions (as measured by circuit training or a 300-yard shuttle run). Finally for players of certain physical types the deterioration can be seen in considerable weight increases.

It is probable that four to six weeks out of training results in a most significant drop in fitness levels as measured by strength and power, so that local and general endurance decreases. This means that the pre-season training period of four to five weeks becomes unnecessarily severe. There also appears to be some support for the contention that the shorter the severe training period, the quicker fitness falls off when the training load drops. Since our early season demands two matches in seven days, for some time, the training loads have to be adjusted accordingly. This would seem to indicate that the concentrated and relatively short pre-season training period must be extended in order that more gradual progress can be made. Concentrated pre-season training programmes may also result in a spate of early-season muscular strains and tears.

In the future the close-season and pre-season arrangements may take the following form:

1. Following the last match of the season there will be a complete break of two weeks.
2. During the following ten weeks the players will be allowed a further two weeks' holiday but these weeks will be taken singly at any time during the months of June and July.
3. From the third week in May until the beginning of July, except where they are on holiday, the players will report at the ground for two half-days a week. On these occasions they

will take part in organized activity programmes lasting for one-and-a-half to two hours. These programmes will not be related closely to specific soccer training. They will be vigorous in content and progressive in intensity although, at this stage, only gradually so. Weekly checks will be made on each player's condition.

4. From the end of June the players will be required to report for a progressively increased amount of training and the training emphasis will move towards specific soccer work.

.5. During the third week in July the player will be approaching full training.

Such a programme arrangement will remove the need for a severe pre-season training period. The training benefits will last longer and, most importantly, there will be no need for conflict to arise between skill and fitness requirements. The order of priorities in all soccer training will be recognized as:

1. Team skill.
2. Individual skill and technique.
3. General and specific fitness.

The arrangement of the present close season and that of close seasons of the future can be represented in the form of graphs (see *figs.* 126*a, b* and *c.* These give an approximate indication of the kind of training to be emphasized in the close season.

PRESENT CLOSE SEASON

Figure 126a

A fairly widespread belief exists in football that players do not become match fit until they have played three or four matches. This belief, in itself, points to the need for a re-appraisal of the close season. On the opening day of the league programme the team should be at peak fitness. As we well know the early-season programme is intensive and therefore early-season results are of paramount importance. The training programmes which follow represent an attempt to come to terms with the demands of modern football organization and competition.

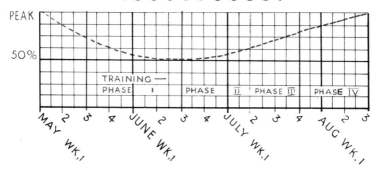

Figure 126b

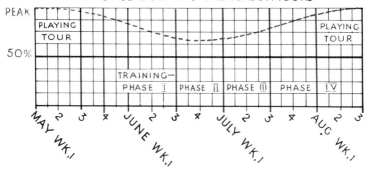

Figure 126c

CLOSE-SEASON TRAINING

Training will recommence two weeks after the last match of the season, and players will be required to attend, in suitably-sized groups, for two half-days each week. Training may then be scheduled in five phases:

Phase I   Commencing at the beginning of the third week in May: two half-days per week.

157

Phase II   Commencing at the beginning of the third week in June: four half-days per week.

Phase III   Commencing at the beginning of the second week in July: three to four full days.

Phase IV   Commencing at the beginning of the fourth week in July: full training.

Phase V   Commencing at the beginning of the third week in August: competitive season training.

One of the advantages of controlled close-season training will be that ball play and practice can proceed without break and without fear of muscular injuries. Much of the training in *Phase I* is based upon enjoyable group competition and the groups of players should be four or six in number. These groups should report on the same half-days throughout this phase of training. When possible the training should be based upon team competitions.

Phase I

Days 1 *and* 2

10 mins. warm-up; 30 mins. minor games: volleyball, basketball, or soccer tennis, or handball; 15 mins. break; 10 mins. warm-up; 30 mins. group competitions: athletics competitions (sprint, hurdles, relays, etc.), or 2 *v* 2, 3 *v* 3 a-side soccer, or soccer skill competitions (e.g. ball juggling); 20 mins. weight training or circuit training.

All activity sessions will be preceded by a warm up of ten minutes or so.

Phase II

Day 1

As for a training session in Phase I. Circuit training will always take place.

Day 2

45 mins. five- or six-a-side football using quarter-pitch; 10 mins. break; 30 mins. individual technique practice; 15-20 mins. weight training.

Day 3

As for a training session in Phase I. Circuit training will be included.

Day 4

45 mins. functional or phase practice; 10 mins. break; 30 mins. individual technique practice; 15-20 mins. weight training.

Phase III

Day 1 (*a.m.*)

45 mins. 11-a-side practice; 10 mins. break; 45 mins. functional practice.

p.m. 45 mins. individual technique practice; 15-20 mins. weight training.

Day 2 (a.m.)
20 mins. team discussion; 60 mins. match practice: four spells of 15 mins. each with 5 mins. intervals.
p.m. 45 mins. individual technique practice; 10 mins. break; 20 mins. pressure training; 15 mins. circuit training and swimming, if possible.

Day 3 (a.m.)
As for training session in Phase I.
p.m. 45 mins. functional practice; 10 mins. break; 25 mins. repetition maze runs, and swimming, if possible.

Day 4 (a.m.)
45 mins. functional practice; 10 mins. break; 45 mins. individual technique practice.
p.m. 60 mins. functional practice; 15-20 mins. weight training, and swimming, if possible.

As the training progresses in duration and intensity the harder training days can be concluded with twenty minutes in a swimming pool. This is not to say that swimming is part of training but that swimming takes the place of massage as a form of hydro-therapy. There will be no swimming after the second week in Phase IV.

Phase IV

Week 1
Day 1 (a.m.)
30 mins. team discussion; 60 mins. match practice.
p.m. 45 mins. functional or phase practice; 10 mins. break; 30 mins. interval maze runs, and swimming, if possible.

Day 2 (a.m.)
20 mins. team discussion; 1½ hours match practice: three spells of 20 mins., one of 30 mins., with 10 mins. intervals.
p.m. 45 mins. individual technique practice; 10 mins. break; 20 mins. pressure training; 20 mins. circuit training, and swimming, if possible.

Day 3 (a.m.)
20 mins. team discussion; 45 mins. functional training; 10 mins. break; 45 mins. phase practice.
p.m. 45 mins. individual technique practice; 10 mins. break; 20 mins. pressure training; 20 mins. circuit training, and swimming, if possible.

Day 3 (a.m.)
20 mins. team discussion; 45 mins. functional training; 10 mins. break; 45 mins. phase practice.

p.m. 45 mins. individual technique practice; 15-20 mins. weight training, and swimming, if possible.

Day 4 (*a.m.*)

20 mins. team discussion; 60 mins. match practice—no interval.

p.m. 45 mins. individual technique practice; 10 mins. break; 30 mins. repetition inter-passing drills; 15-20 mins. circuit training, and swimming, if possible.

Day 5 (*a.m.*)

Recreational activities—golf, tennis, etc.

p.m. As for training session in Phase I.

Week 2

Day 1 (*a.m.*)

20 mins. team discussion; 60 mins. functional practice.

p.m. 45 mins. individual technique practice; 40 mins. repetition skill drills or maze runs.

Day 2 (*a.m.*)

20 mins. team discussions; 90 mins. match practice, 10 mins. half-time.

p.m. 20 mins. team discussion; 45 mins. functional practice; 10 mins. break; 20 mins. circuit training; 10 mins. weight training, and swimming, if possible.

Day 3 (*a.m.*)

20 mins. team discussion; 60 mins. functional practice.

p.m. 45 mins. individual technique practice; 10 mins. break; 20 mins. pressure training; 20 mins. repetitive skill drills or maze runs, and swimming, if possible.

Day 4 (*a.m.*)

20 mins. team discussion; 60 mins. match practice; 10 mins. break; 45 mins. individual technique practice.

p.m. As for training session in Phase I ($1\frac{1}{2}$-2 hours), to include: 20 mins. circuit training; 15-20 mins. weight training; and swimming, if possible.

Day 5 (*a.m.*)

30 mins. 5- or 6-a-side football; 10 mins. break; 30 mins. individual technique practice.

p.m. Half day off or tennis, golf, etc.

Day 6 (*p.m.*)

Match practice.

Week 3

Day 1 (*a.m.*)

45 mins. team discussion; 60 mins. functional or phase practice, at a low work rate.

p.m. 45 mins. individual technique practice; 10 mins. break; 30

160

mins. repetition skill drills or maze runs or pressure training or circuit training.

Day 2 (*a.m.*)

45 mins. individual training practice; 10 mins. break; 45 mins. functional practice.

Evening. 90 mins. match practice.

Day 3 (*a.m.*)

30 mins. team discussion; 60 mins. functional or phase practice.

p.m. 45 mins. individual technique practice; 30 mins. repetition skill drills or as Day 1 of this week.

Whichever form of endurance training is used during week 3 of this training phase will be used for the next four or five weeks. All performances will be timed and recorded.

Day 4 (*a.m.*)

20 mins. team discussion; 60 mins. team practice.

p.m. As for training session in Phase I, to include: 15-20 mins. weight training.

Day 5 (*a.m.*)

45-60 mins. loosening up.

Day 6 (*p.m.*)

Match practice.

Week 4

Day 1 (*a.m.*)

60 mins. match discussion; 45 mins. match inquest team coaching—light work.

p.m. 45 mins. individual technique practice; 30 mins. endurance and speed work (see Week 3, Day 1, p.m.).

Day 2 (*a.m.*)

45 mins. individual technique practice; 10 mins. break; 15-20 mins. weight training.

Evening. 90 mins. match practice.

Day 3 (*a.m.*)

45 mins. team discussion; 45 mins. match inquest, team coaching —light work.

p.m. As for a training session in Phase 1, to include: 30 mins. endurance and speed work.

Day 4 (*a.m.*)

30 mins. team discussion; 45 mins. functional and phase practice.

p.m. 45 mins. individual technique practice; 15-20 mins. weight training.

Day 5 (*a.m.*)

60 mins. loosening up.

Day 6 (*p.m.*)

Match play.

Phase V

During this early season period most clubs are playing two matches each week; the period lasts for approximately six to seven weeks. It is generally accepted that the effects of fully competitive play are difficult to calculate and medical authorities suggest that at least twenty-four hours are needed before the player has fully recovered from competition. On this basis therefore the day preceding a match will be free from anything but the lightest work and the same will apply to the day following. Where it is proposed to play two matches in two or three days, inter-match recovery may well be assisted by light training.

We can now roughly classify our training days as follows:

Heavy: Morning and afternoon (3-4 hours).
Fairly Heavy: 3 hours.
Average: 1½-2 hours.
Light: ½-1 hour.

Naturally we must also take into account the nature of the training carried out. It has been found that training rhythms are important and that interference with the rhythm should be avoided where possible. It should be emphasized, however, that rhythm is used to indicate a fairly consistent pattern of changing intensities in training, not stereotyped and unchanging types of training.

In a training cycle where a team is involved in mid-week matches, taking into account the need for recovery after matches, the following training cycles can be used according to whether the mid-week match is played on Monday, Tuesday or Wednesday.

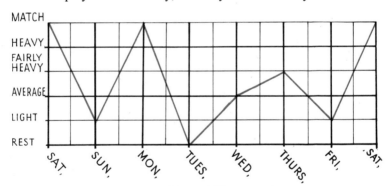

Figure 127

Matches on Saturday, Monday and Saturday (fig. 127)
Saturday—match; Sunday—light training; Monday—match; Tuesday—rest; Wednesday—average training; Thursday—fairly heavy training; Friday—light training; Saturday—match.

Matches on Saturday, Tuesday and Saturday (fig. 128)

Saturday—match; Sunday—rest; Monday—light training; Tuesday—match; Wednesday—average training; Thursday—average training; Friday—light training; Saturday—match.

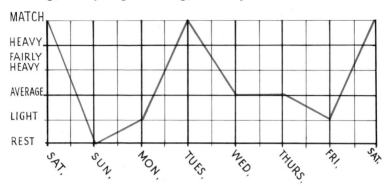

Figure 128

Matches on Saturday, Wednesday and Saturday (fig. 129)

Saturday—match; Sunday—rest; Monday—average training; Tuesday—light training; Wednesday—match; Thursday—average training; Friday—light training; Saturday—match.

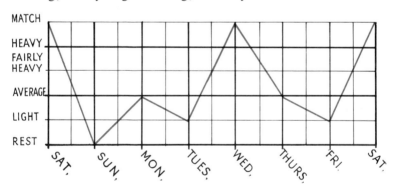

Figure 129

Taking the cycle in which a mid-week match is played on the Tuesday as an example training might be as follows:

Saturday—match.

Sunday—rest.

Monday—$\frac{1}{2}$ hour match discussion; 1 hour coaching team play and match inquest.

Tuesday a.m.—loosening up. *Evening*—match.

163

Wednesday—20 mins. match discussion; 45 mins. functional practice; 10 mins. break; 30 mins. repetition skill drills or 15 mins. weight training.

Thursday—1 hour team play coaching; 10 mins. break; 45 mins. individual technique practice.

Friday—30 mins. team discussion; 45 mins. team practice—light work.

Saturday—match.

It is to be expected that the two match per week cycle will disrupt training but match play cannot substitute for training since the demands of a match can vary for each player. If competitive play could substitute adequately for training and coaching then team problems would be immediately solved. It is vitally important that coaching should be progressive and that factors such as group skill, individual technique, power, speed, and endurance should be developed as far as the demands of the playing programme will permit. It is obvious that the mid-week match programme is a hindrance to the development of players to their fullest capabilities.

TRAINING IN THE NORMAL SEASON

Most clubs will prepare the training programme to reach a peak midway between matches, that is to say on Tuesday or Wednesday. Sunday will be a rest day or, for some players, a light training day. Monday will be an average training day with perhaps two hours of lightish work. Tuesday will be a fairly heavy day with the players working for two to three hours. Wednesday will be the peak of the training cycle with three to four hours. Thursday will see training diminish in intensity and Friday will be a light day.

Monday a.m.

30 mins. match discussion; 60 mins. match analysis—coaching; 10 mins. break; 30 mins. individual technique practice.

Tuesday a.m.

60 mins. functional practice; 10 mins. break; 45 mins. individual technique practice.

p.m. 30 mins. endurance and speed work; 10 mins. weight training.

Wednesday a.m.

90 mins. match practice.

p.m. 45 mins. functional or phase practice; 10 mins. break; 30 mins. endurance and speed work.

Thursday a.m.

60 mins. team coaching; 10 mins. break; 30 mins. endurance and speed work; 10 mins. weight training.

Friday a.m.
30 mins. team discussion; 45 mins. team play—light work.
Saturday
Match.

Where possible all training should take into account changing ground conditions. If heavy grounds are to be played on then training should take place under similar conditions and the same applies to hard or frozen grounds. Where team, functional, or individual skills are part of the training the conditions for practice must be the same as the conditions for play, so far as these can be anticipated. For this reason training indoors is no substitute for training which is carried out under normal playing conditions.

It will be noticed that the same order of priorities has been recognized in the daily programme as was laid down for the whole of training. Team or group skill takes precedence over individual skill which in turn takes precedence over 'fitness work'. Team skill requires, above all things, the maximum amount of attention from players. The aim should not be to work players hard, in the physical sense, merely for the sake of working them hard. They should, however, work very hard mentally. In order that players are able to give this degree of attention the intensive work which is required during fitness training will be carried out at the end of a training session or a training day. Work which is concerned with the improvement of individual technique is placed between team work and fitness work. The time which is devoted to fitness work will depend upon:

1. The quality and intensity of the work.
2. The progressive loading to reach the recommended training distances.

Occasionally, perhaps once a fortnight, the players will undertake fitness and individual skill work before match practice. This will be a useful indication of the extent to which the players can maintain their skill levels when tired. In all training and coaching programmes there must be sufficient flexibility to allow the reaction of players to training to be an important consideration. Training and coaching must fit the needs of players; players should not be required to submit themselves to training merely to suit organization. However, effective training demands hard work; a coach can invent variety and he *must* produce interest, but hard work must always be involved.

TRAINING FOR AMATEUR CLUBS

It will be assumed that amateur clubs undertake training on one, two or three evenings each week. The main problem, therefore, is one of time although the order of priorities must still be observed. A further problem will be posed by the training facilities which are available both indoors and out. If such a club has floodlights and no indoor training accommodation, training will be a straight-forward problem. If, however, there are not opportunities for out-door training, rather bigger problems occur.

1. A club with a floodlit training area equal to the size of half a pitch or a full pitch.

It is assumed that the training time available will be two hours.

Pre-season training

Where possible the players should turn out for one training session a week throughout the close season up to the beginning of July. These sessions will be aimed at maintaining a reasonable standard of general fitness and will take the form as for the professionals in Phase I of their training.

Phase I—*May-June*

Example

10 mins. warm up; 20-30 mins. volley ball or hand ball or hand tennis or soccer tennis; 10 mins. break; 15-20 mins. circuit or weight training, or 30 mins. mass relays and maze runs; 20-30 mins. 1 *v* 1, 2 *v* 2, 3 *v* 3 soccer competitions.

The aim here should be a session of enjoyable activity leading up to twenty to thirty minutes of intensive work, followed by some form of competition such as team games. Where possible, training for amateur or part-time players should be competitive. In other words, the games which are played should be organized on a fairly long-term competitive basis. The short intensive period during the training session should provide the basis for the assessment of fitness. The close season is also probably the best time for players to deal with individual technical weaknesses or deficiencies. It could be that individual technical coaching could take the place of the minor team games during the first forty minutes of a session. Whether this will be so or not will depend on the extent to which individual players *want* to improve.

Phase II—*July*

There will be two two-hour sessions each week.

Day 1

10 mins. warm up with a ball in groups or individually; 60 mins. functional, phase, or team practice (half-hour shooting for

forwards and half-backs); 30 mins. endurance and speed training; 20 mins. small-sided team competitions.

Day 2

10 mins. warm up with a ball; 60 mins. functional, phase or team practice (half-hour shooting practice for forwards and half-backs); 30 mins. individual technique practice.

Since this club is training out of doors, the endurance and speed work will be selected from: repetition skill drills, pressure training, and maze runs.

Whatever selection is made the ultimate target is 1,500-2,000 yards at a high work rate. In other words the basis of the calculation of training requirements is the fitness aspect of training will be as nearly as possible the same as for professional or full-time players.

Phase III—*August*

There will be three two-hour sessions each week.

Day 1

10 mins. warm up with a ball; 60 mins. functional, phase, or team practice (half-hour shooting practice for forwards and half-backs); 35 mins. endurance and speed training; 15 mins. 5- or 6-a-side football.

Day 2

10 mins. warm up; 90 mins. match practice; 20 mins. pressure training (shooting practice for forwards and half-backs).

Day 3

15 mins. team discussion; 60 mins. team practice and inquest; 35 mins. endurance and speed work; 15 mins. individual skill practice or, 5 *v* 5 football; 15 mins. shooting practice for forwards and half-backs).

Where possible the teams would also have Saturday practice matches from the beginning of August until the commencement of the season.

During the competitive season it is assumed that the number of training sessions each week will be reduced to two. Where this is so and where there are no mid-week fixtures, Day 2 in Phase II will become Day 1 during the playing season and either Day 1 or Day 3 in Phase II will be examples of the training which will take place on the second training day during this period.

Many attempts have been made to find an easy method through which training can be made entertaining and effective for casual players. Training can be 'fun' but 'fun' is not necessarily training.

Hard work can be made enjoyable by making it progressive and purposeful. Effective training must be intensive for some of the time but it demands sustained effort. There is no easy way around this particular obstacle.

2. Training for players who have to work in a gymnasium only. Football is played in pre-determined circumstances and there can be no adequate substitute for outdoor training other than that which can take place in large sports halls. Where regular training takes place in a normal gymnasium this, in itself, almost determines the nature of the game which will be played by that particular team. Their game will tend to become a short-passing game which, in itself, is not necessarily a bad thing. Assuming that all main training problems will come with the advent of the early nights, our priorities remain the same except that team skill will relate to 2 v 2 and 3 v 3 soccer.

The groups of players might well be arranged in relation to their functions on the field. If we are working in teams or groups of three these might be: (1) right-back, goalkeeper, and centre-half; (2) right-half, outside-right, and inside-right; (3) left-back, left-half, and outside-left; (4) centre-forward, inside-left, and one other.

Any combination can be used where it brings together players who normally work near to each other on the field.

Working in the gymnasium it is absolutely essential to record activities as an incentive for training.

Example

Two-hour session—24 players.

10 mins. warm up, individual technique practice; the players are shown a sequence of ball juggling movements (e.g. flick the ball onto the left foot, bounce it on the left foot, left knee, then on the right foot and right knee alternately). Set a target number of sequences, e.g. 50, before the ball is allowed to touch the ground; 30 mins. 3 v 3 change football using benches as goals; there are twelve players to each team. Each team of twelve is subdivided into four groups of three. Each group of three is numbered one, two or three. As a number is shouted so the respective teams begin or carry on playing. When the game has commenced the shout of a number does not stop the game but the teams change accordingly and carry on with the game. As goals are scored so they are added to the combined groups' total; 20 mins. maze running or obstacle course relay; 20 mins. soccer tennis (3 v 3) using the four gymnasium beams as nets. Alternatively, benches stacked two-high can be used; 10 mins. individual technique

practice as previously; 10-15 mins. 2 *v* 1, or 1 *v* 1 'keep the ball' competition; divide the gymnasium into three equal zones; 20 mins. obstacle course relay or maze running relay (the alternative to that done earlier).

Three-against-three soccer is extremely useful for coaching an understanding of the principles of the game. If a small number works while the majority watch, a limited amount of coaching of interpassing play can be achieved. Such things as setting-up play, wall passing, blind-side play, movement of the ball, and overlapping movements can be effectively dealt with.

Obviously a large number of players in a small space means that the tempo of training must be lowered. Here it becomes even more important to set aside time for specific and intensive fitness training. In the programme given it should be noted, however, that of the 120 minutes available, two-thirds of the time has been given to group or individual skill considerations.

One of the coach's main difficulties in devising training programmes is the anticipation and avoidance of staleness or boredom. Players can lose interest in training or even in playing for that matter, for many different reasons. Thus variety in training is important but it must not become the basis for training; progressive work would become impossible because the coach would rarely be in a position to measure results. Variety may provide entertaining training but this does not necessarily mean effective training. A further danger occurs when the variety introduced involves sustained muscular contraction in a relatively new anatomical position. For example, anyone who has taken part in 'duck fighting', where players in pairs try to shoulder-charge each other off balance while in the full crouching position, will know what is meant by stiffness. This sort of thing introduced occasionally as variety in training is dangerous, since it usually results in a severe degree of stiffness, certainly enough to affect a player's performance for two or three days. New work must be introduced very carefully and gradually and with a great deal of thought as to its ultimate effect.

3. Training for players who have to train alone

Generally speaking very few people are capable of sustained training efforts lasting from one and a half to two hours when working alone. This being so, a player who finds himself in this unfortunate position is well advised to train for sixty minutes four times each week. It is important that he produces a detailed training schedule and records it as it is completed. This schedule should lay down exactly what he intends to do for each minute of the time available. He should also honestly record his reaction to the training and how much effort he puts into each part of it. Training under these difficult circumstances demands great concentration and the organization of time can help to achieve this concentration.

Since the player is unable to take part in team or group practice he will have to offset this deficiency in skill by working harder during the game. His skill will not be as economical as that of other players since he is not in a position to develop it through training and practice.

Suggested training schedules

If some form of rebound surface (e.g. a wall or a fence) is available this will help considerably.

Day 1 (60 mins.)

5 mins. warm up; ball-juggling sequences; 20-25 mins. control and passing or control and shooting techniques: (1) starting forty yards from the rebound point, the player kicks a high ball in front of him. He then runs and controls the ball quickly to shoot or pass against the rebound surface. Collecting the rebound he dribbles as fast as possible back to his starting position. On his return he may set himself a problem of dribbling around two or three real or imaginary obstacles; (2) running parallel to the rebound point giving and receiving wall passes to beat an imaginary opponent; (3) Standing ten to fifteen yards from the rebound point, serve against the wall, control the rebound with one touch and volley or half-volley the ball against the wall; (4) Chip the ball against the wall so that it passes, on its return, over your head. Turn and control the ball before it bounces three times. Dribble back to the wall and repeat the sequence; (5) Using two footballs and starting forty to fifty yards from the rebound surface, dribble both balls along by rebounding one ball off the other from varying distances. If the first ball misses its target collect the second ball and carry on. The pace of the pass has to be well judged since a hard pass which misses its target means a long run to retrieve it. At a suitable distance from goal, the player shoots one ball, controls the rebound and dribbles both balls back to the starting line. Finally, 10 mins. circuit without apparatus.

The player will establish his training load and rate in exactly the same way as it is done for a full apparatus circuit. A recommended circuit might be as follows:

170

(1) Trunk curls: test to maximum in 60 secs.; (2) Squat thrusts: test to maximum in 60 secs.; (3) High press-ups: test to maximum; (4) Shuttle run (10 yards): test to maximum in 30 secs; (5) Dorsal raise: test to maximum in 60 secs; (6) squat jumps: test to maximum in 60 secs.; (7) Sit-ups: test to maximum in 60 secs; (8) Crab walk (10 yards): test to maximum in 60 secs.

Having tested himself to find the greatest number of repetitions of each exercise in the time recommended, the player halves each total (e.g. total number of sit-ups in 60 secs. might have been 52. The player's training dose is, therefore, 26). Following the exercise programme, as detailed previously, the player carries out the training dose for each of the recommended exercises until he has done all the exercises from 1-8. This single run through should be done as fast as possible. Since he will go through the circuit twice without stopping, the initial target time can be twice his single circuit test time. He will then work to improve this time for a period of three or four weeks. After the training period he will retest his performance and establish new training loads and rates. Next, 20 mins. repetition running with a ball.

Using the markings on a football pitch, if one is available, this might be as follows: start at one corner; run across the field behind the goal keeping the ball up, other than with the head, all the way; walk from this corner to the half-way line, keeping the ball up with the head; from the half-way line to the next corner an all-out sprint with the ball; working across the field from corner flag to corner flag, easy jogging with the ball; from the next corner-flag to the half-way line, a high kick followed by quick control and dribble; from the half-way line to the starting point easy walking.

The various field markings can be used in many ways. For example, on reaching the goal-line edge of a penalty-area, the player may push the ball across the area and then run around the outside of the area to collect the ball before it passes outside the penalty-area on the far side. The intervals of light work to fast running with the ball should start in the proportion 3:1 and, as fitness grows, progress to 1:1. The aim is to produce a comparable degree of effort intensity to that which has been outlined in the previous training methods.

In the case of a player training alone, boredom is a major problem and, therefore, as much of the work as possible will be done with a ball. The circumstances for which these schedules are devised are looked upon as the worst possible. If any additional possibilities occur such as an opportunity to train with perhaps one other player or to take part in weight training, perhaps once a week, so much the better.

Day 2 (60 mins.)

5 mins. ball-juggling sequences; 20-25 mins. selection of the skill practices outlined in Day 1; 30 mins. fartlek training using a ball. Fartlek means speed play. The player varies the speed and nature of his work by mixing very fast work with slow work and changing from perhaps short intensive periods to sustained half-pace efforts. The important thing is that he does what he feels capable of doing while he is actually training. Generally speaking an athlete undertakes this work in open or wooded countryside and he uses natural hazards to train against. For example, if he comes to a hill he will sprint up the hill, perhaps even a number of times. Using a ball the same principle can be applied in any large field. Here is a 30-minute example: (1) 5 mins. easy-paced running with the ball; (2) 30 secs. all-out sprinting with the ball followed by 60 secs. jogging with the ball (perhaps keeping the ball up but allowing it to bounce once after each contact with it). The number of such work stints might be six giving a total of 9 mins.; (3) 5 mins. fast walking: tap the ball ahead, catch it up before it stops rolling; (3) 30 secs. of close control dribbling involving frequent stops, starts, full turns, and changes of direction. Again the 30 secs. of work will be followed by 60 secs. easy jogging or walking. The toal number of repetitions might be four or six; (4) Finish with 3-5 mins. of three-quarter-paced running with the ball. Some players break up the fartlek run by doing body exercises perhaps every 5 minutes or so. These can be those which have been recommended as exercises for non-apparatus circuit training.

Once again it is most important that a player keeps a record of the training work which he is doing. It is easy to delude oneself into thinking that training is effective when this is far from the case. Even a feeling of tiredness does not indicate, necessarily, effective training. Certainly perspiration is a poor indication.

These training days are then repeated for the following two days in the training schedule. Monday's work Secomes Wednesday's and the Thursday programme is the same as Tuesday's.

The question often arises, how much does playing other games help in training for soccer? This question is best answered by asking "How intensive is the game?" Squash racquets can be excellent as part of soccer training. It demands agility, power, and endurance of a high order but only when your opponent is capable of extending you. If he isn't, you can play and use no more energy than in a game of golf. Training aimed specifically at any game cannot be adequately substituted by any other game or activity.

TRAINING FOR GOALKEEPERS

One of the main deficiencies of any programme of mass training has been attention to the goalkeeper's problems. He is in a unique position on the field of play and his requirements are entirely different from those of any other player. The general endurance requirement, for example, is of a low order. It is difficult to imagine a game sufficiently prolonged in intensity to exert significant stress upon the heart-lung mechanism of a goalkeeper. His running speed requirement is also of a low order: a goalkeeper is rarely required to run significant distances at speed.

However, running speed must not be confused with speed of movement, or agility. A goalkeeper needs great agility, that is, the ability to change direction and his body position in the shortest possible time.

Power is a fundamental requirement of any goalkeeper. He may be called upon to jump in any direction as far and as fast as he possibly can. The explosive character of jumping is as good an illustration as any in fact, of power.

It is often said that a goalkeeper must be 'acrobatic'. To be acrobatic a goalkeeper needs to be supple and strong, supple to enable him to assume unusual positions in flight and on the ground, strong because these positions are demanded of him unpredictably. He must do what is demanded of him by the game; he cannot do what he wants when he wants. Finally, of course, a goalkeeper must be able to understand and read the game as well as any other player. His passing of the ball must compare with that of any half-back or inside-forward.

A goalkeeper's technical requirements are, of course, peculiar to his position, and training and coaching must take this into account. Assuming that his skill can be catered for in functional, phase, and match practice, as it is for any other player, the following changes should be made in the general programme of training to suit his special needs. We can omit the speed and endurance items immediately; a goalkeeper's time can be better spent. He should however, take part in circuit training and weight training; the former to develop all round toughness and general condition; the latter as the basis for the development of power. Weight training should be a permanent and regular part of any goalkeeper's training.

173

AGILITY TRAINING

Using an open goal (i.e. without nets) in an area where there is up to twenty yards of space in front of and behind the goal. Three to five players with a ball each

Two servers stand in front of goal facing the goalkeeper (*fig.* 130). Initially the service will be the same from each of the two servers. For example, they might begin by throwing the ball at just above head height but aimed slightly to one side of the goalkeeper. The

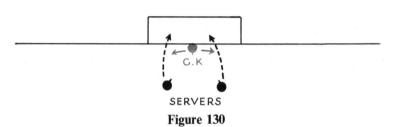

Figure 130

goalkeeper catches each service and returns it to the server. As he becomes accustomed to the routine the balls are served at the same height but increasingly further away from him. Each service must be delivered at a speed that expedites his release of the previous ball; he must be made to react quickly but always with a reasonable chance of making the save.

This exercise can be varied by throwing alternately at head height and along the ground. A final variation might be unpredict-

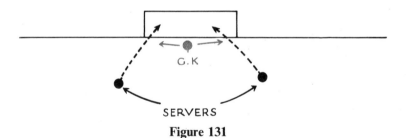

Figure 131

able balls from both servers. The servers might also move into much wider serving positions (*fig.* 131) so that the goalkeeper cannot watch both at the same time.

The practice can then be changed so that one server is in front of the goalkeeper and one behind him. This makes him change his basic position quickly for each save. Again, while one serve is being made the blindside server changes his position perhaps five yards to right or left of his central starting position (*fig.* 132).

If the goalkeeper fails to make a save then the original server retrieves the ball while the other server keeps the repetition of service going. In a group of three there should always be one spare ball to allow this to happen.

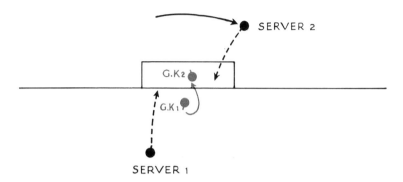

SERVER 2

G.K2

G.K1

SERVER 1

Figure 132

Using the same basic arrangement the goalkeeper may be required to adopt an unusual starting position before making the next save. For example, he can develop agility in recovering from a kneeling or even a full lying position. As he makes a save and returns the ball he must resume the kneeling or starting position each time. Moving quickly from difficult positions is part of a goalkeeper's job. To make this test even stiffer, two or three other players can be used to partially unsight him while the save is being made.

When pressure training develops to a point where all the services are kicked rather than thrown, so more players will be needed.

In *fig.* 133 the goalkeeper has three service possibilities. From player A he receives a ball which is crossed from a wing position. He must catch it or punch it clear. From player B he receives a low drive, and from player C he receives an angled drive between knee and shoulder height. Player D is a target man for all goalkeeper clearances and also for the retrieved balls from E and F behind the goal. Player D keeps A, B. and C cupplied with footballs. The repetition of service is always the same. A, B, and C in that order. It must be emphasized that the servers are required to shoot in the way which is specified and they are doing so in a controlled manner in order to extend the goalkeeper. In other words, the aim is not

175

shooting practice but goalkeeper practice. Occasionally he can be tested to the full but generally speaking he should be just able to save as the practice reaches peak intensity. This form of work is very severe and provided that the repetition of service is unbroken, peak intensity should not be maintained for more than two minutes. After a rest of the same length of time, the practice can continue with periods of work followed by periods of rest. If

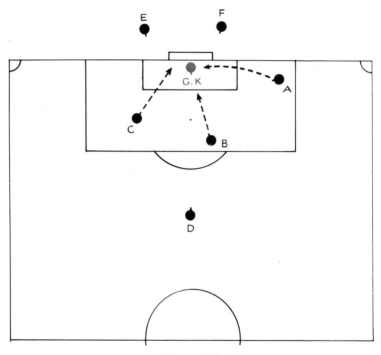

Figure 133

additional players are available they can be used to unsight the goalkeeper or indeed to offer challenge after he has made the save. There are many variations of pressure training which can be used.

Where goalkeepers have to practise singly or in pairs a rebound surface is vital. This can be a wall or a meshed throwback structure A large sandpit in which the goalkeeper makes his saves is extremely useful since it reduces the possibility of injury and, at the same time, it produces a form of resistance training. In jumping or diving the goalkeeper has to work very hard to move at speed or to jump reasonable distances since the sand does not provide a firm base for a push off. This sort of work will improve a goalkeeper's jumping movements.

Where two goalkeepers are working together the following practice has been found to be successful.

Player A, the goalkeeper, stands facing the wall or rebound surface, initially three to four yards away from it. Player B stands behind player A and serves the ball against the wall by throwing it. Player A cannot see how much pace there is in the service nor can he see the ball's angle of approach to the wall until late in its flight, since he must watch the wall all the time. As he becomes increasingly proficient, player A moves nearer to the wall thus denying himself time in which to make the save. By varying the angle of his throw, the server, player B, can test player A's reactions in jumping to make saves in all directions.

MOBILITY TRAINING (SUPPLENESS)

A goalkeeper needs to be supple in all the major joint complexes of the body and for the purpose of devising suitable exercises and activities we can classify these joint complexes as follows:

1. Neck and upper back in all planes.
2. Shoulders in extension.
3. Lower and mid back in all planes.
4. Hip in all planes of movement.

In every training session the goalkeeper should spend twenty minutes on suppling or mobilizing work. The longer a goalkeeper neglects suppleness the more difficult the problem becomes.

1. *Exercises for the neck and upper back*
   (a) Reach forward with the head rubbing the chin as far down the chest as possible. Keeping the chin on the chest and subsequently on the neck, lift the head as high as possible.
   (b) Stretching the neck as far as possible, neck rolling so that the chin describes as large a circle as possible.
   (c) Punching forward with alternate fists, as the right fist comes forward twist the neck to look over the right shoulder. As the left fist punches forward twist the neck to look over the left shoulder.

2. *Shoulders*
   (a) Kneel sitting, hands stretched out in front, press the body as close to the ground as possible so that the fingers can reach forward on the ground—a little further each time.

177

(*b*) Back lying, knees bent, feet and hands flat on the ground with the fingers pointing towards the feet. Press up on hands and feet until the body is fully arched and the head is clear of the ground.

(*c*) Lift the arms above the head and place the fingers of each hand on the spine behind the neck. Bend the arms backwards to allow the fingers to reach further and further down the spine.

3. *Lower and mid back*

(*a*) See exercise 2 for shoulders.

(*b*) Lying on the front, using the hands, push the head and upper body upwards and as far backwards as possible.

(*c*) Standing, place the left hand behind the right thigh and try to slide the hand as far down the thigh as you can. Repeat using the right hand on the left thigh.

(*d*) Back lying, lift the legs overhead so that the feet touch the ground behind the head. Walk as far back as you can with the toes touching the ground all the time.

4. *Hips*

(*a*) Standing crouch, hands flat on the ground, two feet in front of the toes. Keeping feet and hands still push the knees straight. Move the hands back towards the feet a few inches each time.

(*b*) Hurdle sitting. Sitting with one leg out straight in front and the other leg bent so that its knee is at right angles with the front leg. Alternate head pressing to the front knee and the side knee. Change leg positions and continue.

(*c*) Standing facing a fence about three feet high, place one heel on the fence and press the head down to touch the knee of that leg. Change legs and continue.

Suitable games for goalkeeper training are: volleyball—depending on the number of players so the court can be made to suit the number; or basketball, or the same game using a different goal such as tower ball with a skittle, or sentry ball. These can be played with as few as two players on each side.

Here is suggested a goalkeeper's training session lasting two hours: 5-10 mins. easy warm up; 60 mins. functional, phase or match practice with the other players; break; 20 mins. agility practice; 20 mins. suppling work; 10 mins. weight training.

PART III

*Definition and
Acquisition of Skill*

9 Skill

The process through which players learn and, equally important, the process through which a coach can cause players to learn efficiently are vital to improvement in standards of skill. Before we can consider some of the factors involved, however, we must attempt to define skill in soccer. In the past, skill has been closely associated with high levels of performance in the so-called basic techniques of the game such as heading, kicking, tackling, dribbling, etc. It was held that the basic problem in teaching or coaching the game was establishing a level of competence in these techniques. In other words, the problem was approached by reducing or simplifying it into what were held to be its component parts. This, of course, was true of all sports coaching, indeed some sports still hold firmly to the belief that if the coach and the player pays attention to the fundamental techniques of the game a commensurate improvement of his performance in the game will follow.

Our present knowledge in skill psychology indicates certain shortcomings in this belief. In the first place, it is reasonable to assume that the skill of soccer is different from the skill required by other activities. Some sports will have certain factors in common with soccer, others will have little or no similarity. In some games the techniques of the game almost correspond to the skill of the game. Billiards is a good example. Here a player has the problem of putting a ball into a pocket. The problem is solved if his potting technique is good which is a matter between himself, his cue control, and the ball. In other words, the skill environment is simple and predictable. In Association Football the problem is complex and the environment largely unpredictable. The player needs accuracy and control in hitting the ball but his targets are moving, unlike those of the billiards player, and even more importantly, his opponents are able to interfere with his intentions by a considerable variety of methods not least of which is physical challenge. Clearly a billiards player will gain considerable benefit from repetitive practice of technique since the practice situation bears a high degree of similarity to the competitive game. The same sort of practice for soccer, however, would overlook the testing circumstances of competition. Soccer skill requires the application of techniques in a situation where the player has co-operative possibilities and, at the same time, is opposed by one or more players. These factors require him to make decisions and the ability to make correct decisions is probably the most important single factor in developing skill at the game. It follows, therefore, that practice situations must include these elements. What are some of the more important considerations which will affect the coaching situation?

MOTIVATION

All players, like all coaches, are as different as human beings and they bring their individualities to practice and to the game. They must be encouraged to do so. A coach must understand his players as individuals and, particularly, he must try to understand what each player wants to achieve as a player. Players know their capabilities and their limitations; the coaching problem is to find out what the possibility of improvement means to each player. The assumption, for example, that professional players are highly motivated because of financial rewards and that these rewards will result in an improvement in skill, is not necessarily accurate. The basic drives towards improvement are established long before there is the remotest possibility of financial reward. A coach who takes the trouble to find out what his players want to contribute to the game is laying a foundation which is vital to successful coaching. This is not to say that the player is always entirely right but it is fair to say that understanding his thinking is the only sensible way of changing it.

INTEREST

There is a widely held belief that people who have developed a reasonable degree of competence in a sport will be interested in learning to become better at it. This belief is only partially true; it seems probable that initial interest will be given readily but that a player's subsequent and continued interest will depend upon the ability of the coach to meet the player's individual needs. This is why mass coaching involving large numbers of players taking part in repetitive, highly controlled practice cannot be effective. The greater the player's experience the more this will be true.

The development of interest is closely related to motivation. A coach must prepare his training programme for the generation and regeneration of interest. In the first place, he must explain the purpose of the work and continue to explain it. Players must be encouraged to discuss the programme's content and its success or failure. A coach who causes players to conform to a training programme without understanding it is encouraging disinterest. But an interesting programme must not be confused with an entertaining one. An entertaining programme may be interesting, for a time, but it may have little or no purpose. We must accept that some players will be difficult but these players must be looked upon as a challenge to a coach's ability not rejected as being beyond contact.

INCENTIVES

Sustained interest depends upon the extent to which a training programme is effective. A coach must be prepared to measure training achievements, record them, and discuss them with the players. Targets or standards cannot be absolute: they will vary from individual to individual. Some players respond well to difficult targets, others to targets' which barely extend their abilities. Learning is not a steadily progressive and predictable process. Some players react well to long periods of hard practice, others will only produce high quality work in training for relatively short periods. Hard physical effort is no indication of the effectiveness of practice for the development of skill but all skill practice must be of the highest quality.

Short periods of work at maximum concentration followed by short rests or changes of activity appear to promote more effective learning. There are strong indications that there is an unavoidable mental time lag in a learning process which is an integral part of it. Players should be educated to come to terms with it. After all, some will learn rapidly and others will show a less immediate response.

Training targets may be evidence of the coach's effectiveness but the ultimate test takes place in the game. Even here assessment can be fairly objective: an observer can easily be trained to observe and record a player's performance in a match, particularly if he is only observing one aspect of the player's performance. This assessment can be made of any aspect of play and when carried out fully is

known as match analysis. This statistical analysis of a match or a
player can, when interpreted by a coach, provide an accurate
diagnosis of strengths and weaknesses.

SUCCESS

Coaching must always be positive. Players need to understand
what they should do. Merely to tell them what they should not do
is mainly negative, destructive, and depressing if continued for any
length of time. Generally, players respond well to a feeling of
success since they will want to repeat the feeling. They will avoid
a situation in which they feel that they may be unsuccessful even
though that particular situation is one which may be vital to a
successful development of play. A coach cannot have fixed standards by which a player's success is judged. He will have ideals but
these cannot be learning targets for each player. This is not to say
that a coach must always praise, this is unrealistic and continuous
praise loses its value. Constructive criticism is important but,
generally, praise is more important than criticism. A coach who
looks for every opportunity to give credit to a player is likely to
have the player on his side. The player becomes interested because
he has been shown to have been relatively successful. As a consequence his motivation is increased. This is as true of the inter-
national player as it is of the schoolboy.

So far we have been concerned with the inter-action between
the personalities of the coach and the player. Coaching and learning
are human problems basically but there is a growing body of knowledge which can be advantageous to us in the field of skill psychology. Earlier in this chapter some consideration was given to the
fundamental factors in soccer skill. A coach must measure the
value of his work by what takes place in the game. In other words,
if what he attempts to put over in practice circumstances is immediately apparent in the next game, he has been 100 per cent
successful. This is how a coach measures his effect.

COMMON ELEMENTS

The circumstances in which skill practice takes place must correspond as closely as possible to the circumstances in which that
skill is to be used in competitive play. There are many players who
have developed a high degree of technique in ball manipulation
whose performance in the game is not at a comparable level. The
performance of soccer techniques outside the game is one thing; the
reproduction of these techniques in a competitive game is another.
Thus, in devising practice situations we must analyse the circum-

stances in which a player is required to exercise skill in the game. The factors which can be isolated through such an analysis must be included in the practice situation.

1. The player may receive the ball in various ways. In practice, therefore, we must reproduce different types of service to order.
2. The player's performance in the game may be affected by direction. He either plays towards a goal or away from a goal. Direction and, if possible, some sort of goal must be a part of practice. There must be some clear aim to the practice to give it purpose.
3. When receiving the ball, a player may have other players or at least one other player with whom he can develop his skill. In practice there must be at least one team mate.
4. When receiving the ball in the game a player may be challenged by one or more opposing players. Opposition must be a part of the practice situation.
5. In a game a player may make a choice from various techniques such as heading, controlling, and the different techniques of passing. In practice we may need to limit choice of technique but choice of subsequent action should be open to him.

Making the right decision is important and decisions are most closely affected by opponents. This serves to re-emphasize the importance of factor (4) in devising practice. All these factors must be reproduced in coaching sessions although some control may be imposed by varying the time or space which a player has at his disposal during practice.

REINFORCEMENT

It seems to be an inherent part of the learning process that a player needs an experience to be repeated before it is fully explored and mastered. The full game is so fluid and unpredictable that the likelihood of a situation repeating itself in match practice is remote. But repetition for the sake of repetition may only be of limited value. Players do not play by habit and intense repetitive practice of the same situation is likely to condition a player's thinking too narrowly. The value of a practice situation depends on the extent to which a player's understanding of it is developed. We are, in fact, concerned with developing a player's awareness of the possibilities which are open to him.

The whole of this chapter has emphasized the need for skill to be treated as a whole matter rather than a number of isolated parts.

It is of considerable importance that a player should understand why a certain aspect of play is necessary as opposed to merely being shown how it is achieved.

MENTAL SKILL LEARNING

We cannot separate the mental from the physical in developing skill. It seems probable that the exercise of skill is more of a mental process, in some ways, than the physical act suggests. There is every indication that some skill learning takes place unaccompanied by physical practice. Barriers to progress may be overcome by frequent rest periods during which, as we have already seen, the mind catches up, as it were. Mental rehearsal of a skill problem appears to have some advantages although the extent to which this process is effective is not yet fully understood. It does serve to show, however, that skill is not merely a physical involvement and that coaching and learning are by no means simple logical processes.

The solution of skill problems is much the same as that involved in doing a jig-saw puzzle. The full picture is studied and the relationship of the various parts to each other. The puzzle is reassembled with a continuous reference back to the full picture. The player is exposed to various possibilities and then discovers through guided experience the most satisfactory decisions to make.

PROGRESSION

In the past coaching proceeded through pre-determined progressive stages. The nature of progression usually related to the degree of difficulty of the practice. We progressed from the easy to the more difficult and so on. The decision as to when progress should be made and more particularly the nature of the progression will be indicated by the player. Learning is not predictable and logical, certainly not so far as speed or rate of learning is concerned. Occasionally we overcome learning barriers by going back to easier situations. It is also possible for barriers to be over come by going forward, for a short period of time to a much more difficult situation. One thing we can be certain of is that coaching must be flexible enough to allow each player to take what he can from the practice situation when he can. Learning does not proceed by a series of rules.

DEVELOPMENT OF PRACTICE

The coach should attempt to make the need for coaching apparent to the player by reference to his performance in the game where some competitive situation may have exposed a deficiency in the player's performance.

1. All coaching should begin with some form of realistic competitive situation.
2. When the aspect of play in which deficiencies have been noticed occurs, the coach should stop the activity and recreate 'the picture' in which he has noticed the deficiency.
3. The coach should then set up a demonstration of 'the picture' offering, or requiring the players to offer, alternatives. This demonstration may be in shadow form, that is to say, without opposition, since at this stage we are working for a clear understanding of ideas.
4. A group of players then demonstrate the actual practice situation while the coach and players suggest alternatives. Encouraging the players to express their own ideas is of major importance. They know their limitations better than anyone.
   Practice is repeated and the group returns to a fully competitive situation periodically.

A coaching session using the above principles might be as follows. The coach has noticed his team's inability to give short accurate passes.

1. 6 *v* 6 small game or attack against defence (time: five to six minutes).
   (*a*) Coach emphasizes the need for supporting the player with a ball in all phases of the game.
   (*b*) The coach stops the practice to show 'a picture' of situations in which the short pass can be most effective.
2. The coach or a player demonstrates the technique of push-passing, emphasizing the principle of the technique (time: two minutes).
3. Working in threes the players try the various techniques using the inside of the foot, the outside of the foot or a combination of the instep and the outside of the foot (time: two to three minutes).
4. The coach sets up a practice situation involving three or four players probably in a small area. Player A has the ball and stands 10-15 yards from his partner. Player C marks Player B but stands 10 yards away from him. The goal towards which A and B will play might be a line in which case they score a goal if they can progress to the line so that one or the other of them finishes with one foot on the ball on the line.

Alternatively, the goal might be represented by two posts perhaps two yards apart at first, through which A and B attempt to push the ball. It is important that there should be an end result to give direction and purpose to the practice. The practice proceeds as follows: A must push the ball forward once before trying to pass to B. As soon as he touches the ball for the first time both B and C become active. C moves in to try to intercept the pass or to tackle B as the pass arrives. Depending on the first pass, A and B interpass or dribble to score a goal.

As A becomes better at measuring his passes, C is allowed to stand nearer to B at the beginning of each sequence. At the same time scope is created for A to pass behind C if he comes towards B too quickly. The provision of at least one alternative in any practice situation is important since it allows A to make a realistic decision about the skill which he uses. When this occurs, C must be allowed to choose whether or not to tackle B or whether to feint to tackle and then to hold off. Again this degree of freedom of action will cause A to take it into account when deciding what pass to give. Once the initial pass has been given the coach is then in a position to emphasize certain aspects of passing technique as he observes the need and, at the same time, he can coach for combined play. An opportunity may occur for a wall pass. Similarly an opportunity may occur for dealing with the correct weighting of a pass. Coaching develops according to the demands of the players and as a result of experience; it is not imposed unrealistically. As players improve so the practice can involve bigger groups. The only artificial aspect of such practice is at the beginning where the opposing player is restricted in terms of distance. The situation might be likened to stopping and restarting a film. Occasionally it may be advisable for the coach to take all the players through a certain aspect of play in slow motion, as it were. This process must include all the players, those who are opposing as well as those who are combining against them. Here the coach is attempting to gain an understanding of his requirements (time: twenty minutes).

Following a rest or a change of activity, the players return to the original practice arrangement of a small-sided game, attack versus defence or some similar competitive situation where the openings for the application of push-passing in giving short accurate passes would be re-emphasized as play demanded it.

Occasionally, and for short periods, a 'condition' might be imposed on the game to emphasize this particular technique. Such a condition might be that all passes must be on the ground. Failure to observe the condition results in a free-kick or the award of a point to the opposing side (time: twenty minutes).

The application of technique is far more important than technique itself. Technical weaknesses can be solved by developing a player's appreciation of the situations in which certain techniques are best used from his own point of view. As a result the player's confidence is raised and he is prepared to attempt further advances.

IMAGINATION

All practice is artificial to a greater or lesser extent. A coach's ability to stimulate the imagination of players is obviously of importance in making practice worthwhile. Very young players naturally create an imaginary world through which experience becomes meaningful. As players grow older, real experience takes the place of fantasy but it is likely that adults retain some ability to create interest through the powers of imagination. Where players are able to undertake and gain benefit from isolated repetitive technical practice, it seems that transfer of training may be affected by their ability to imagine a relationship between their practice and the game. Imagination of this order may be rare, as rare as those players who can reproduce, accurately, a complicated skill after one demonstration of it. Coaching gifted players can be as difficult as coaching players at the other end of the scale. Gifted players require a great deal of ingenuity from the coach in order that they are extended. This is another reason why groups of players must be treated as individuals. There is a considerable range of learning ability in any team group. It does not follow, however, that the quick learner automatically becomes the top-class player. The complexity of the many factors involved in reaching the summit is vast. Not least of these must be a burning desire to become a top-class player. The psychology of high-class competitive performance is an almost untouched field of study. When we know a great deal more about it we shall have overcome a major coaching obstacle.

10 Coaching and Teaching Techniques

PASSING AND KICKING

It is often said that if a player cannot pass the ball he cannot play the game. What should be said, of course, is that if a player cannot pass the ball accurately it is unlikely that he will be effective in the higher levels of football. The higher the class to which he aspires, the greater degree of control and accuracy which will be required of him.

We can classify passing techniques so far as the feet are concerned as follows:

1. Those which are on the ground, and
2. Those which are lofted or in the air.

1. GROUND PASSES

In this technique various surfaces of the foot can be used but, as keeping the ball on the ground is the main requirement, they have principles in common.

(a) To keep the ball on the ground the line of force must be through the mid-line of the ball or above it (*plate* 8). The more the point of impact descends below the mid-line, the greater the likelihood of the ball being lifted.

(b) To make such an impact possible the foot should be at the lowest point of its swing as impact is made. This is facilitated when the knee is over the ball. The further the player is behind the ball, the more his foot will tend to swing upwards. Similarly, if the player is too far over the ball, his foot will tend to be on the downswing and, consequently, will tend to squeeze the ball into and off the ground.

(c) In achieving accuracy, the longer the foot can follow through in the direction of the target, the more chance there is of accuracy. The same condition would apply to hitting any ball, whether it is in cricket, tennis, or golf.

(d) The degree of power is determined by the speed at which the foot is travelling as it strikes the ball. The leg is a lever: the longer the lever, the more powerful the effect. However, in this technique, where the ball is to be kept on the ground, it is difficult to obtain a long leg-swing and make the impact

Plate 8

Plate 9

which is necessary to keep the ball low. Here a second lever, formed by the lower leg hinging from the knee joint, is used. Accelerated speed of foot is achieved by striking the ball by an explosive straightening of the knee. This can be done with the knee over the ball in the case of the low drive (*plate* 9), or level with the ball in the case of a pulled drive, which is a more powerful version of it.

Plate 10   **Plate 11**

Common passing faults. The player 'sits' as he attempts to push pass. This can cause:

(a) The ball to be struck below the mid-line and thus lifted.

(b) Lack of power in the pass.

(c) Such a position means that alterations and adjustments in technique cannot be made. At the same time it places the player in a badly balanced position.

(d) The swing of the player's leg is across the ball rather than through it.

Some techniques seem to contradict general principles, for example, the flick pass with the outside of the foot. Here the player deliberately stands to one side of the ball so that he is sideways on to the direction of the pass. He then 'throws' the front outside edge of his foot at the ball with a whip-like movement of the leg. The knee leads followed by the ankle, followed by the rest of the foot, each straightening in quick succession (*plate* 10). Since it is very difficult to position one's knee over the ball in this technique, it is of the utmost importance that the point of impact is right. In fact most players, when making this pass, impart top spin on the ball since their foot tends to pass from the mid-line upwards while contact is being made. The same considerations apply when a toe pass is made. Accuracy of contact is the most important factor.

Backheeling (*plate* 11). By the very nature of this technique, the player is compelled to adopt a position in which all the above principles are emphasized.

2. THE LOFTED PASS

This is intended to pass over an opponent or a number of opponents and may carry for a relatively short distance, in the case of a chip or a short volley, or for a longer distance in the case of a powerfully driven pass. Long passing, where it is used with accuracy and timing, is an important weapon in the armoury of attacking play. It is used from all parts of the field and by all players from the goalkeeper to the outside-left. The greatest effect can be achieved when a team is capable of changing its game from short passing to a sudden and surprise use of accurate long passes. The emphasis must always be on accuracy. The longer the pass the greater the distance covered in one movement, but also the more time available to opponents moving to intercept it. A team which bases its game upon passes of fifty yards or more demands an extremely high level of skill from its players, not only those who are required to deliver the passes but also from those who are intended to receive them.

The long lofted drive. In this technique the surface of the foot which is used is the inside of the instep unless deliberate swerving of the ball is intended. This technique will be considered later. The principles involved in the technique of the long lofted pass are as follows:

(*a*) The line of force should be through the lower half of the ball, upwards and in the direction in which the pass is intended to travel. The last point may seem to be a statement of the obvious but in correcting errors it is of major importance.

(*b*) The second factor is a powerful leg swing. In order to achieve this the approach run is at an angle to the direction in which the pass is intended to travel. The last stride which results in the final placing of the non-kicking foot is a long one. This long stride opens the legs automatically and permits a long swing of the kicking leg. The angled approach run assists in providing a long swing and it also allows the hips to be used as a powerful pivot as the swing begins.

(*c*) The non-kicking foot is planted slightly to one side of and behind the ball. The body begins to lean backwards as the swing of the kicking leg develops. The position of the non-kicking foot ensures that the kicking leg is fully extended as

192

impact is made with the ball and that the kicking foot is beginning to travel in an upwards direction. Distance is a direct result of the power developed during the leg swing. This is generated by:

    (i) the pivot of the hips,

    (ii) a powerful forward swing of the thigh,

    (iii) a final and powerful straightening of the knee just before impact is made.

(d) The point has already been made that the follow through must be a full one and in the direction in which the pass is required to travel. The lean back of the body allows a full follow through to take place. Where the follow through does not take place as a direction pointer, the player will often find that he tends to 'pull' the ball. In the case of a left footed kick the pass will arrive to the right of the target player and the reverse will be true of the right footed kick. It is most important that the player kicks right through the ball rather than at it.

(e) The location of the target player, together with his speed and direction of movement, and the assessment of space and the disposition of opposing players, takes place before the kick begins. From the commencement of the kick, the kicker concentrates on developing the right amount of power and making the most accurate contact with the ball. This means that his eyes are fixed firmly on the ball during the actual kicking movement and they remain focussed on the same place even after the ball has gone. It is worth comparing the techniques of golf to the techniques of soccer in this respect.

The principles of long lofted passing thus are:

    (i) The point of contact between foot and ball is below the mid-line of the ball. The lower the contact the greater the height and, at a certain point, the less the distance.

    (ii) The inside of the instep is used and the ankle must be extended but firm.

    (iii) The non-kicking foot is to the side of and behind the ball (*plate* 12).

    (iv) The approach run is angled.

    (v) The last stride to plant the non-kicking foot is a long one.

    (vi) The leg swing is as long as possible and begins with a hip pivot.

    (vii) The knee is straightened powerfully before impact is made (*plate* 13).

(viii) The kick is made through the ball and is followed by a full
follow through (*plate* 14).

Common faults in lofted passing. All players go through phases
where their techniques, or some of them, appear to be letting them
down. The following are common faults:

Plate 12

Plate 13

Plate 14

COACHING AND TEACHING TECHNIQUES

(a) Where there is power without accuracy, the kicking foot may tend to wrap round the ball slightly. This results in the ball being 'pulled'. This may be because the run up is rather straight, and can be corrected by exaggerating the angle of the run-up. It may also be caused by opening the kicking stance too soon. This means that the player has used his hips too soon and that usually the full front of his body can be seen before the actual kicking movement has been completed. A third reason may be that the kicker is casual in controlling the direction of the follow through meaning that he has probably been casual about the kicking contact with the ball. This is shown when the kicking leg swings across the body and, therefore, across the line of the pass too early.

(b) If there is insufficient height in the pass, the foot has hit the ball slightly too high perhaps due to a player lifting his head while the kick is being made. Lifting the head results in a slight straightening of the body and probably a slight raising of the kicking foot.

(c) Where height and direction are good but power is inadequate, the player may be kicking at the ball rather than through it. He may also be sitting back as contact is made which can be caused by taking too long a stride into the kick or by placing his non-kicking foot too far behind the ball. This faulty technique prevents the weight of the body from being transferred though the kicking movement into and through the ball.

(d) Where too much height and not enough distance or 'carry' is obtained, the foot is being applied too far under the ball during impact which means that since the ball has been directed upwards, horizontal force is being wasted.

When a player finds that he is pulling his long kicks he can often adjust by slightly exaggerating the extent to which the shoulder, corresponding to the non-kicking foot, points and remains pointing in the direction of the target or target player.

The 'chipped' pass. This is used to gain height steeply over a relatively short distance. When a chipped pass lands it should check. There are two ways in which this can be achieved.

In the first the full instep is used and, to gain maximum height, the impact between instep and ball is made on the under surface of the ball. To achieve this the toe of the kicking foot is stabbed beneath the ball and through the ground, usually taking up a piece of ground in the process. The ankle is not extended a great deal and is held firm. Because of the natural curve between ankle and instep and because the impact is aimed at the lowest possible point on the

195

ball's surface, the line of force is much nearer to the vertical than the horizontal. At the same time the ball is caused to spin backwards during flight. This achieves two purposes: it assists the ball to gain height and, on landing, causes the ball to grip or to hold the ground rather than to run on. The speed of the kicking foot is developed almost entirely by a quick straightening of the knee which is not completed until after the ball has gone. The approach run is almost in line with the intended direction of the pass. The non-kicking foot is close to and level with the ball and there is little, if any, follow through. Accuracy of contact is vital in this technique and the head is kept down throughout the movement. This type of pass is best achieved when the ground is soft enough to allow a piece of the ground underneath the ball to be removed during the kick or when the ball is already rolling towards the player as he makes the chipped pass. The movement of the ball allows the player to get his kicking foot immediately beneath the ball. The most difficult circumstances in which to produce a chipped pass are when the ball is rolling away from the kicker or when the ground is extremely hard.

The second method of chipping involves an angled approach to the ball or, alternatively, the toe of the foot is outwards and away from the direction of the pass as the ball is kicked. This means that the lower part of the instep and the upper part of the toe of the boot is the only part of the foot to make contact with the under surface of the ball. The foot is swept rather than stabbed beneath the ball. The purpose of both techniques is to reduce horizontal force and make contact with the ball as far beneath it as possible. So far as back spin and, therefore, holding is concerned the first method appears to have greater advantages.

Common faults in chipped passing

(*a*) The player stands too far behind the ball or, alternatively, does not allow the ball to come close enough to him when he attempts to stab or sweep his foot beneath the ball.

(*b*) If the ball is moving away as he attempts the chip he fails to strike beneath the ball fast enough to compensate for the fact that the ball is moving away. In this situation difficulty arises because he is trying to convert a forward rolling of the ball into back spin.

(*c*) He fails to keep his head down. Lifting of the head causes the whole body to straighten and tends to cause the kicking foot to lift also. This results in ball contact being made rather than a contact immediately beneath the ball. This explains the tendency for such a kick to cause the ball to

196

Plate 15

travel horizontally rather than to climb steeply and 'hang' in the air.

(*d*) Too much follow through in the kick which causes some contact with the ball by the instep. This, again, makes the ball travel horizontally to an unrequired extent.

VOLLEY KICKING

The volleyed pass is made while the ball is in the air; it can be short or long. The principles of kicking still apply in as much as the greater the power required the greater the need for a long leg swing. This degree of power can be achieved in two ways.

In the first the player waits until the ball is as near to the ground as possible before kicking. This allows him to develop his leg swing in much the same way as he does for the long lofted kick from ground level. Since the ball is off the ground, he will have to lean slightly away from it in both a backwards and a sideways direction as he swings his leg. The higher the ball is when the volley is attempted, the more this 'lean away' will tend to be exaggerated in order that he can develop a leg swing and, at the same time, swing his foot in the direction in which he wishes the ball to travel (*plate* 15). If the player continues to adopt a position in which his target, the path of the moving ball and himself are in line the higher

197

Plate 16   **Plate 17**

the kick will tend to travel. In these circumstances the height at
which the ball is contacted will determine the amount of power
which is available. The higher the ball the less he can use a full leg
swing. He must use increasingly. whatever power is available by
swinging his kicking foot from the knee. Of course, the higher the
ball, the greater the difficulty in stretching the ankle so that the
ball is struck by the instep. Most players use the falling or leaning
away technique when volleying since this allows the kick to be
made early and with the maximum amount of power available.
This technique is vital when shooting on the volley since the shot
has to be kept reasonably low.

THE SHORT VOLLEY

This pass can be made with any part of the foot other than the toe.
In the main, most top-class players deliver it with the instep or a
part of the foot between the instep and the outside of the foot. Very
little full leg swing is used and the movement is brought about by
using the knee almost exclusively. This allows a pass to be made
over a very short distance or a fairly long one since the swinging
action at the knee joint is free and natural. Balance is important in
this technique (*plate* 16) since the position and stability of the non-
kicking or standing leg provides the basis from which the volley

can be made. The use of this short lever, from the knee downwards, allows the player to exercise a great deal of control which is the foundation of accuracy.

The short volley can also be made with the inside of the foot by turning sideways to the direction of the pass. The range of passes made in this way is very limited and the technique is almost always used for short passing to a nearby colleague. The pass is given by a short swing of the thigh caused by pivoting the hips. The knee is usually bent at right angles and held firm and the same is true of the ankle. The latter position allows the biggest and flattest striking area of the foot and ankle to be employed (*plate* 17).

The volleyed pass can also be given by flicking the ball away using the outside of the foot. This technique is almost identical with that of the flicked ground pass described earlier except that almost all the movement comes from the knee and ankle.

Common faults in volleying are mainly related to the position of the kicking foot at the moment of impact and the position of the body while the kick is being executed.

In the former case:

(*a*) The ankle may be loose when it should be firm.

(*b*) The ankle should be extended in order that contact is made with the instep (the exception is the pushed volley with the inside of the foot).

In the latter case:

(*c*) The higher the ball is from the ground when the kick is attempted, the more the body must be leaned away from it. The direction of the body lean is, roughly speaking, at right

Plate 18

angles to the path of the ball and the direction in which it is intended to travel. Leaning away from the ball permits the kicking leg to be lifted to a height which is as near to being level with the ball as possible. This in itself permits a ball to be kicked with a lower trajectory.

(d) Leaning away also permits a full leg and body swing into the actual kicking movement.

THE OVERHEAD KICK

This technique is merely an extension of the technique described previously. The body leans fully backwards in the direction in which the ball is intended to be kicked. As the trunk falls backwards, the hips may be raised if a powerful overhead kick is required (*plate* 18). The lower the hips the less will be the amount of kicking power available.

A really powerful overhead kick, for example when shooting, may involve a mid-air kick after a jump. The jump enables the kicking leg to be as high as the ball at the moment of impact which means that the ball has a low trajectory. This type of overhead kick is often best executed when the ball is kicked backwards over the player's shoulder by the opposite leg. In a left-foot shot, for example, the player would use his left leg to kick the ball over his right shoulder by using a scissor kick. This can be an effective technique for a surprise attempt on goal when any other attempt would require too much time. The player will almost certainly land on his back with only a small chance of breaking his fall.

THE HALF-VOLLEY KICK

The half volley is made as the ball touches the ground. All surfaces of the foot can be used and whether or not the kick or pass stays on the ground depends upon whether the player observes the principles of ground passing technique or the principles of lofted passing technique. The most effective use for a half-volley kick is where a player has to deal with a ball which approaches him in the air and from which he wishes to give a ground pass to a colleague without having to stop the ball. In making such a pass the player's contact with the ball must be accurate since the slightest error will produce a miskick. The player must be well over the ball in a position which will enable him to watch the ball onto the ground. The kicking movement involves a fairly relaxed sweeping movement of toe, foot, and leg and contact is made slightly above the mid-line of the ball to ensure that the ball is kept low. There is little, if any, follow through after contact with the ball has been made.

Common faults in half volleying

    (*a*) Failure to judge accurately exactly where the ball will bounce. It is necessary that the non-kicking foot should be in position as near to the ball as possible before it strikes the ground.

    (*b*) Too much follow through during the kick which causes the resultant pass to be lifted.

    (*c*) Failure to strike the ball above its mid-line.

    (*d*) Failure to watch the ball all the time during its approach and failure to keep the head down while actual ball contact is being made.

SWERVING THE BALL

The ability to cause a pass or a shot to swerve is a useful technique and most players at all ages know what is involved sometimes without realizing it. One frequently sees a player attempting a straightforward corner-kick when he produces a kick which swings or swerves away from goal. So far in our analysis of kicking and passing techniques, we have considered the position of the kicking foot in relation to the mid-line of the ball which is parallel to the ground. If we now consider the vertical mid-line of the ball we can see how swerve is imparted.

We can take low driving as a simple example since the principles involved in swerving a ball on the ground are the same as those for swerving a ball in the air. In straightforward low driving, contact is made through the centre of the ball. This causes the ball to travel straight and low. If, however, we strike the ball slightly left of centre, as we stand facing it, the ball begins to spin in a forwards direction from left to right, that is, in a clockwise direction. If we strike the ball to the right of the centre the ball spins in the opposite direction. The ball swerves in the direction of spin. The two varieties of swerve can be produced using the same foot, for example, here is how it would work with the left foot: to swerve the ball from left to right the instep is wrapped around the left hand side of the ball as contact is made; to swerve the ball from right to left the ankle is turned inwards so that the contact surface of the foot is partly the instep and partly the outside of the foot. Contact is made on the right hand side of the ball and the foot is swung vigorously across the body and, therefore, across the ball. The approach run for such a kick tends to be much more in line with the ball and the target than for the previous technique.

To produce the same result in the air (e.g. for a corner kick) the contact between foot and ball takes place towards the required side but, at the same time, below the horizontal mid-line of the ball according to the amount of height required. It should be realised that the spin which causes a ball to swerve in the air also causes a reversal of direction when the same ball hits the ground. This is why goalkeepers can be tricked by a high swerving shot which lands in front of them. Swerve causes the ball to move in one direction through the air while spin causes the ball to move in the opposite direction off the ground. This change of direction is perhaps more evident in top-class off-spin bowling in cricket. The ball swings or swerves away from the wicket during its flight and spins towards the wicket after it pitches.

Swerving a pass round a defender is a technique which is often used in top-class soccer but it is difficult to control by the receiver. Whenever passing or kicking to a team mate our job is to make the problem of controlling the ball as easy as we can for him. Any player who goes onto a field with the intention of making things as easy and as simple as possible for his team mates is well on the way to becoming a very good soccer player.

HEADING

Although, at its best, soccer is played mainly on the ground, the technique of heading is vital. At times, and particularly against well

Plate 19   **Plate 20**

organized defensive play, it may be necessary to play the ball over defenders rather than risk playing through narrow and well guarded gaps on the ground. Provided the technique is introduced at an early age, most boys will quickly gain a great deal of satisfaction out of mastering the ball in the air. Certainly there can be few experiences more spectacular and exciting than the centre forward leaping to head a goal. At the same time, heading is a technique which may be something of an exception so far as the general principles of coaching are concerned. Early experiences can be painful if careful progression in building up confidence is not applied.

1. *Where the player is on the ground*

   (*a*) The feet provide the base from which power and control are developed.
   (*b*) The player may face the ball, with his head and chest square to it (*plate* 19), or he may adopt a position in which he stands rather sideways on to the approaching ball (*plate* 20). In either case a wide position of the feet will allow a considerable movement of the trunk backwards and forwards.
   (*c*) The ball is hit with the flat frontal part of the forehead (*plate* 21). This part of the head is well protected by bone and also gives the most accurate striking surface.
   (*d*) The head is thrown towards the ball by the powerful muscles of the legs and trunk and is continued through a vigorous nodding movement of the neck and head (*plate* 19). As in all

Plate 21   **Plate 22**

striking actions the player should head through the ball and continue the follow through in the direction in which he intends the ball to travel.

It is most important that the head should hit the ball. Where players allow the ball to hit the head a considerable jarring can be caused which is extremely painful. The player must dominate the ball at all times.

(*e*) To change the direction of the ball the head and neck are turned so that contact is still made with the same part of the forehead.

(*f*) The decision to head the ball must be made early, whenever possible, in order that the head and neck can be cocked ready for the controlled and powerful striking movement.

2. *Where the player is in the air* (*plate* 22)

(*a*) The jumping take off should be from one foot. In achieving maximum height in a jump the principles which apply to the high jump technique in athletics apply here. The stride onto the take off foot is a long one with the body leaning back. The weight rocks over the take off foot from heel to toe. As the take off leg extends powerfully the other knee is swung forward and upwards equally powerfully. A forward and upwards swing of both arms will assist momentum.

(*c*) To cock the trunk, head and neck ready for heading, it is recommended that after take off both legs should be kicked backwards and upwards. This causes the whole spine (of which the neck is part) to arch backwards. From this position in which the player appears to hang in the air, the upper body is jack-knifed forward at the hips and the normal snapping forward of the head occurs.

(*d*) The timing of the jump so that maximum height is gained as the ball arrives is extremely difficult. The great headers of the ball, Dean, Lawton, and in more recent times, Kocsis of Hungary, and Jones of Tottenham and Wales, appear to jump and hang for a period of time in the air. Such a feat is, of course, impossible, but the illusion occurs because these players are able to time their jumps to a split second. It seems probable that most players tend to jump slightly late but as with all techniques, success will follow practice.

As a final consideration of technique, the part played by the eyes is important. Although it is likely that the reflex blinking action causes the eyes to be closed at the moment when the ball is struck by the forehead, players should be encouraged to watch the ball right onto the forehead. Only by doing so can a player time the actual heading movement accurately. There need be no fear of danger to the eyes since they are well protected by the heavy bone structure immediately above them.

In jumping to head a high ball, particularly when maximum height is required, the single foot take-off after a short approach run has been described. On occasions, however, a player has no time in which he can prepare to jump, therefore, a standing jump is forced upon him. The problem here is in overcoming inertia and whenever possible the player should be moving, however slightly, if he is likely to receive the ball. This applies to all circumstances in which the ball may come to him but particularly when he is likely to have to jump off both feet.

Footwork is therefore of double importance. In the first place it is used to ensure that a player is in the right position at the right time. In the second place any movement of the body assists in overcoming the inertia of the player's body weight. If this principle is questioned players can test it in the following way: smear the fingers of one hand with chalk and from a position in which the feet and body are still, jump to touch as high up a wall as possible. Then try the same jump with the feet still but with preliminary bouncing movements of the body. Finally perform the same jump with one or two preliminary small bounces using the feet and the body.

BACK HEADING

This technique may be used by a forward to make a surprise attempt on goal when he is standing with his back towards it. Similarly, when heading forwards might allow an opposing player a shot at goal from close range, a defender dealing with a high ball may decide to head backwards to a team mate or to the goalkeeper.

1. The ball is played with the upper part of the forehead where the forehead begins to slope back onto the top of the head. This allows the ball to be played firmly and also the ball may be watched for as long as possible. Where contact is made further back on the head the player cannot see what he is doing and equally importantly, the more painful the experience is likely to be. The movements of the head, neck and trunk are exactly the opposite of those used in the forward heading movement (*plates* 23, 24 *and* 25).

2. Obviously, the degree of control in this technique is limited and its only real advantage is in surprise.

205

Plate 23

Plate 24

Plate 25

DEFLECTION HEADING

This is often used by a forward when the ball is played to him at speed. He may wish to deflect the ball without reducing its pace much. His intention may be to deflect the ball slightly away from a defender in order that another attacker can run on and collect the ball in his stride. The deflection required may be so fine that to use the full face of the forehead would be almost impossible.

1. The ball is played with the side of the forehead where the forehead forms a corner with the side of the head.
2. The head itself is hardly moved at all and the ball is allowed to glance off it. This glancing nature of the technique reduces the possibility that it will be painful.
3. Some players develop a flicking technique with the side of the head which is a combination of power and deflection heading. This produces a result which is difficult to anticipate and is often effective in taking a headed shot at goal from a fast cross. Opposing players are left in doubt as to the direction of the shot until the last moment. They are not sure whether the forward is going to play the ball with the full face of his forehead or whether he is going to deflect or, as is often the case, he will use a combination of the two.

COACHING PRACTICES IN HEADING

For young players and using a light plastic ball.

1. In pairs, pull the ball onto the forehead releasing the ball as the head strikes it. This gives the player the feel of the correct impact. Using this method the players practise heading the ball in different directions: up in the air, down onto the ground, or aimed at their partner's chest.
2. The target player moves through ninety degrees either way, the other player tries to head the ball so that his partner can catch it or trap it. The change of direction to be achieved by turning the body but keeping the feet still. The forehead is used all the time.

THE PENDULUM BALL

A ball is suspended from a bar by a piece of cord. If possible the bar should be adjustable to allow different techniques at varying heights to be practised. Although the path along which the ball travels is almost the reverse of that travelled in free flight, the pendulum ball allows the player to control the speed at which the

207

ball approaches him. It permits aspects of technique to be isolated and it allows a progressive build up of confidence and control.

The next stage involves heading a ball which is in free flight and, where possible, the player should serve the ball for himself. In this way he is able to subject himself to whatever difficulty he is likely to encounter.

1. A throws up the ball and heads to B; B offers his hands as a target at varying heights.
2. A throws the ball against a wall and turns to head to B who is standing to one side of him.
3. A heads to B who traps the ball and passes it back to A. If the header is a good one control is easy; if it is a bad one control for B is difficult.
4. (a) A and B stand behind lines three to five yards apart. Each player serves for himself and the ball is not allowed to touch the ground between the lines. See how many headed passes can each pair make in two minutes.
   (b) Standing in hoops three to five yards apart. Make as many passes as possible in two minutes. If a player has to leave his hoop to catch the ball the sequence is broken and the players must begin again.
   (c) As above, but the ball must bounce once in the space between the lines or hoops.

HEADING FOR DISTANCE

A serves for himself standing on a line. He is allowed three attempts to head the ball over his partner. Where the ball lands, his partner stands. See how far back a player can drive his partner.

Control. In pairs keep the ball up for as long as possible. A serves to B who heads against the wall, controls the ball as it rebounds and passes back to A.

Pair practices of this nature where we are concerned with building up confidence must exercise the player's imagination and, where possible, should have a competitive flavour. As soon as the players show confidence in making contact with their heads, the technique can be applied in simple competitive practices:

1. A serves to B who heads to C. B and C interpass to keep the ball from A. A is allowed to move to challenge for the ball as soon as C touches it for the first time.
2. As above, but A can move to challenge as soon as B heads the ball. A is a fixed distance away from B but C can move where he wishes.
3. If A is finding it too easy to interfere with the combination of

208

BC put in another player. A serves to B who can now head to either C or D. B, C, and D interpass to keep the ball from A. In this way the players are being compelled to judge the application of heading technique in co-operating with players. At the same time this judgement must take into account the movement of an opposing player. As a result of what occurs the teacher can then begin to mould the players' ideas of football. Technique is thus transformed into skill. The target of the two or three co-operating players may be to keep the ball for six uninterrupted passes; if the practice takes place in a ten-yard square, space is restricted and thus opportunity occurs for training in the use of space.

In these competitive practices the nature of the heading technique to be used can be determined in the following ways:

1. *Back heading*. A serves to B who must back head the ball to C who is standing behind him. B and C versus A then becomes a live practice as before. The same arrangement can apply to deflection heading although this technique should be introduced only when players have reached a fairly high level of confidence.

Obviously a most important factor in using these practice situations to the best effect is the nature of the serve. Generally speaking the two handed underarm throw allows the greatest degree of control. The aim of the server is to produce a certain kind of throw thereby helping the other player to practice a set technique. Variations in the service will occur as players become more adept at mastering techniques. Ultimately, where basic football technique is sufficiently advanced and, therefore, controlled, all practices will commence with a ball which has been kicked.

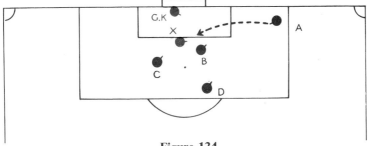

Figure 134

2. *Heading for goal*. Three attacking players, one defender, one goalkeeper and the server (*fig.* 134).

A throws the ball high towards the penalty-spot where B and C are standing, one in front of and one behind the defender X.

D is allowed to take up a position anywhere in the space towards the edge of the penalty area. The service is served with a marked advantage to B or C who can head for goal or head back to D for a shot on goal. X can make whatever attempts he likes to challenge for the ball. B and C are thus placed in a situation where they have to make decisions quickly not only relative to the possibility of scoring but also with a view to heading to colleagues who may be better placed. As skill improves so the margin of bias towards the attackers can be reduced. Occasionally the server will serve a ball which may be low and fast or which bounces some way in front of the group of three. This occasional strange service tests the reactions of the players who must be prepared at all times to deal with any eventuality. The mere mechanical repetition of practice is not enough. Players, even very young ones, must be accustomed to making decisions quickly.

Further practices might be as follows:

(a) A serves to B who has a choice of heading for goal or heading a back pass to an unmarked player. There are four other attacking forwards, two of whom are marked and two of whom are free. The two who are marked must be tightly marked all the time. All the players concerned are allowed to move wherever they wish. B is opposed by a defender but

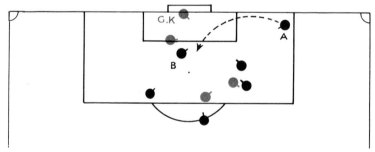

Figure 135

the service is very much in B's favour (*fig.* 135). Here again the player B must select from a number of possibilities. At the same time the marked players are encouraged to think of movements which will clear the way for B to play to his unmarked team mates should B wish to do so.

(b) A and B are attacking players waiting at the far corner of the goal area. C is a defending player. These three players are allowed to move about freely although they know that the ball will be served to the area in which they are standing. A or B try to tempt C into a position which will enable A or B to head at goal (*fig.* 136).

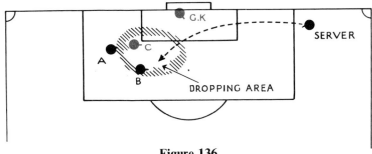

Figure 136

A might pretend to run towards goal while B runs behind him for a clear headed shot. The server will again vary the service to suit the attackers to begin with. As they become increasingly successful so the service will give C a more even chance.

As above with an additional defender, D, and an additional attacker, E.

Here the service may be to A or to E. E can either head for goal, back head the ball towards A or head the ball back towards B for a shot. For A a service to him can lead to a direct headed shot, a headed pass to B or a cross goal header to E. All players are unrestricted in their movements from the moment that the ball is served.

A situation may occur where an attacking player shows that he lacks a certain technique. In the situation above it may be that E cannot back-head the ball effectively. Here we will give him a brief unopposed experience where the server serves to him and he practises the back header three or four times merely to gain the feel of the technique. The teacher or coach will draw his attention to one or two major factors in the technique. As soon as the player shows that he has the idea of the technique he will return to the activity opposed practice circumstances. Experience in live practice situations is more important than polished technical excellence achieved in circumstances which are not related to the game.

4. *Defensive heading* (*fig.* 137). A serves a high ball to B who has the opportunity of heading to his goalkeeper C or to a wing half back D. An opponent X can move wherever he wishes and can

threaten to challenge C or D at any time. B then has to make a decision in relation to the flight of the ball, the possibilities offered by C and D and also in relation of the threatened challenge of X. The addition of a defender and attacker make further complications in this game, if variety is desired.

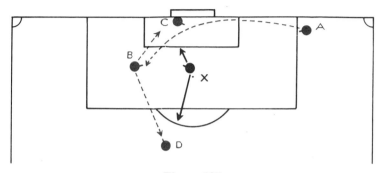

Figure 137

In devising such practices, the coach should use his memory to recall the general pattern of the game. All that he needs to do is to reproduce, in practice form, a play situation. The only adjustments necessary are to the service and to the number of attackers or defenders according to the player towards whom the practice is directed. The accent must be on choice, decision, and live situations.

SMALL GAMES IN WHICH TECHNIQUE CAN BE EMPHASIZED

These minor games are not a substitute for practice based upon game situations. They do, however, provide interesting and enjoyable forms of activity in which the technique of heading can be practised.

1. *Head tennis.* A tennis court or badminton court may be used. For the former seven-a-side can be played; for the latter three-a-side. Generally speaking the net should be at chest height although the higher the net the greater the need for well-timed jumps from players who are in a position to 'smash' at the net. The ball is served from behind the base line in the right-hand corner by a volleyed or half-volleyed kick to pass over the net into the opponents' court. The ball is allowed to touch the ground once only in each court. The ball may be played once with any part of the body by one player only. After this the ball must be played with the head. A team may play the ball five times in its own court but not twice

212

in succession by any one player. The fifth contact, if five plays are used, must result in the ball passing into the opponents' court. Scoring may be the same as for table-tennis or volleyball.

2. *Wall tennis.* Various forms of wall tennis or wall ball have been developed, even football squash played on an actual squash court; provided this is played with a high bouncing ball, it is a most energetic and rewarding game. The wall version is played as follows: The ball is served from the service box onto the wall and

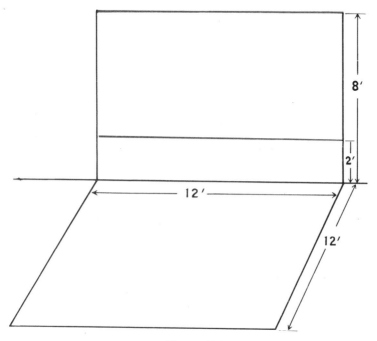

8'

2'

12'

12'

Figure 138

between the red lines (*fig.* 138). It is allowed to bounce once only for each player within the ground court. A player may play the ball a maximum of three times with any part of his body other than hand or arm but the third of such a series of three plays must cause the ball to hit the wall court. Whenever the ball is played against the wall it must be by heading the ball. Each player plays the ball in turn. A player can only win points while he is serving. When he loses a point on service the service goes to his opponent. Any ball striking the wall or ground outside the marked court is out of play and that point is lost.

3. *Sentry ball.* This game is best played with five- or six-a-side on a rectangular court 25 yards × 15 yards. Each team tries to get the ball into its sentry's hands. The sentry stands on a mat or within a marked zone perhaps six feet square. No other player from either side is allowed in this zone and the sentry is not allowed out of it. The passing sequence is throw—head—catch, and no player is allowed to move when he is holding the ball. All other players can move without restriction. No player is allowed to play the ball twice in succession. For example: A throws to B who heads back to A or to another team mate who can catch the ball. The sequence continues using any combination of players until the ball is headed into the sentry's hands. Opposing players can intercept the ball in any way but no body contact is permitted.

BRINGING THE BALL UNDER CONTROL

As the modern game has developed it has speeded up and team play has become highly organized. The time in which a player must receive and bring the ball under control has decreased. As a result, control has to be executed quickly and any part of the body, other than the hands or arms, must be used to control the ball. The classical techniques of trapping the ball between some part of the foot and the ground are still important but increasingly, the need is evident for controlling techniques whereby the ball is 'killed' in the air, possibly requiring the use of head, chest, thigh, or instep. Some of these techniques will be considered in detail but the coach and the player must look for a basic principle by which the entire problem of stopping a ball can be dealt with. The principles of stopping the ball, where the intention is to cause the ball to drop or stop at one's feet, under immediate control, are simple and few in number.

1. Where possible the player should be as close to the line of flight of the oncoming ball as possible. This means that foot-work is important; a player who refuses to move into position and prefers to reach to control the ball is taking unnecessary risks. A goalkeeper should, if possible, place the whole of his body behind the ball when trying to stop a shot. The same principle must apply to the other players. The more difficult the circumstances, the more these principles hold good.

2. The player should decide, as soon as possible, how he intends to stop the ball. The greater his skill the more he will be equipped to change his mind. The lower his skill level the greater the need for an early choice.

214

Plate 26

Plate 27

3. That part of the body used to stop the ball should be as relaxed as possible.

4. Before the ball strikes the stopping surface, that surface should be withdrawn in the direction in which the ball is travelling. Points 3 and 4 are thus aimed at absorbing the pace of the ball. Failure to relax the stopping surface and to withdraw it before impact will cause the ball to bounce away out of control.

These principles are involved whenever a player wishes to cause the ball to come under his control as near to his standing position as possible. If the intention is to control the ball and, at the same time, move off in a different direction certain minor changes in technique are required.

TRAPPING TECHNIQUES

1. *Sole of the foot.* The ankle of the trapping foot is cocked, or bent upwards, so that the sole of the foot is sloping forward at an angle. The angle should be large enough to allow the ball to fit into the space between the foot and the ground (*plate* 26). The ball is allowed to strike the ground and the foot at the same time. The knee is slightly bent and the whole leg relaxed and, as the ball makes contact with the foot and the

215

ground, the foot is withdrawn slightly to cushion the impact. This movement tends to cause the ball to spin backwards slightly thus ensuring that it stays under control.

2. *Inside of the foot*. Here the trapping angle is made by turning the body slightly sideways to the oncoming ball and raising the trapping leg backwards (*plate* 27). The 'trap' is now formed by the inside of the foot and ankle and the ground (*plate* 28). As the ball makes contact with the foot and the ground at the same time, it has passed the standing foot and again the force of impact is cushioned by relaxing the trapping leg and withdrawing it.

3. *Outside of the foot*. This technique, generally speaking, is only used when a player wishes to trap the ball and move off with it in a different direction at one and the same time (*plate* 29). Where it is used to bring the ball under immediate and close control, perhaps by a full back who wishes to trap the ball and turn away from goal, the following technique is used. The trapping leg is stretched out and the foot is turned outwards. The 'trap' is formed by the outside of the foot and ankle, and the ground. Since the ball is travelling in the same direction as the player and he may have his back partially turned towards it, the ball passes the player before it makes contact with the player's foot and the ground simultaneously. The principles of absorbing the shock are applied as previously.

Plate 29

Plate 28

Plate 30   Plate 31

CONTROLLING THE BALL IN THE AIR
(*Plates* 30, 31, 32, *and* 33)

The parts of the body which can be used are the head, chest, thigh, inside of the foot, and outside of the foot. The actual technique is exactly the same for all. The stopping or controlling surface is in line with the flight of the ball and is moved towards it. As the ball approaches the stopping surface is withdrawn and relaxed to absorb the impact (*plate* 32). One of the major faults in using these techniques is that the player anticipates the arrival of the ball too soon. For example, in trying to control the ball with his chest he will find that his chest or trunk has been bent backwards before the ball arrives, with the result that when it arrives he cannot bend any further backwards to take the pace out of the ball. In these circumstances the ball bounces away and out of control.

PULLING THE BALL DOWN (*plate* 30)

This technique is particularly useful when dealing with a ball dropping vertically. The controlling foot is raised beneath the dropping ball and as the ball arrives the foot and leg are lowered. The

217

Plate 32   **Plate 33**

player attempts to 'catch' the ball on his instep. If the ankle is relaxed as the leg is lowered this technique is most effective in 'killing' the ball.

TRAPPING AND MOVING

As a player progresses in football it becomes increasingly necessary for him to trap the ball and move away from the place at which he trapped it, at the same time. Good defenders have a habit of arriving as a player attempts to bring the ball under control. For all the stopping techniques mentioned, as the ball arrives, the stopping surface is turned in the direction in which the player wishes to move off with the ball. The stopping surface is not so relaxed but held rather firmly. Instead of withdrawing the stopping surface the player moves it gently towards his intended direction of travel. This means that some of the force of impact will cause the ball to rebound in the required direction. The player must be balanced and prepared to move after it quickly. In fact, in many cases, he will already be moving in that direction before the ball makes contact with him.

TAKING PACE OFF THE BALL

This technique is used to control a firm ground pass, particularly when a player wishes to turn at the same time. The player turns slightly sideways to the oncoming ball and presents the full surface of the inside of his foot and ankle to it. As the ball arrives the controlling foot is withdrawn and continues to withdraw as the ball strikes it. At the same time the player spins or pivots on the standing foot. This means that, at one and the same time, he is controlling the pace of the ball, reducing it, and turning. Where players are tightly marked in a game this ability to control a ball closely and turn while controlling it is of supreme importance.

STOPPING PRACTICES

1. Working in pairs, one ball between two: A serves, by throwing the ball, to B who attempts to control the ball and hold it while being challenged by A. A's challenge can be unrestricted except by the distance between A and B. If the object is to give B practice in controlling dropping balls, the distance between A and B must be increased or the moment at which A begins to run towards B delayed. If this is not done, A arrives where B is standing before the ball. With inexperienced and young players we can restrict A's challenge by making him hold back until B touches the ball for the first time. Different services can be used by A whereby B must use different parts of his body in controlling the ball.
Part of the skill of stopping the ball involves doing so against a challenge and also doing something with the ball when the controlling movement has been completed.

2. Working in threes with one ball between three players: A serves to B who tries to control the ball. C, who is some distance from B (this distance will depend upon how proficient B is in controlling the ball; the better he becomes the shorter the distance), challenges him for the ball and B can now use A as a team mate. We have thus created a basic two against one situation in which B has to control, knowing that his control will be tested by C's challenge but also having an opportunity to pass to A to get himself out of difficulty. A and B can then try to make three consecutive passes against C or perhaps attack a goal of some kind. With players who are learning, the thrown service is more easily controlled. With experienced players the service will usually be kicked. In other words every opportunity will be taken to increase the realism of the practice situation.

3. The imagination of the players can be stimulated by creating a picture of a situation in the game where a certain stopping technique might be advantageous. The practice begins with two against one as before, and develops with the progressive addition of other players.

The movement of challenging players must not be restricted other than in time. When they are allowed to challenge, the nature of the challenge must be of their own choosing. In this way the player who is having practice has to react realistically and make decisions which involve the whole skill of the game. He cannot do what he wants to do in his own time.

4. Where a wall is available valuable stopping or controlling practice can be obtained using one ball and two players. The ball is kicked or thrown against the wall by A who controls it. As soon as the ball is thrown, B can challenge A for possession. A can then hold the ball against B's challenge and use the wall to play rebound or wall passes against him. Alternatively, B can serve the ball against the wall to test A's quickness in reacting to different angles and heights of service. This means that A must choose the appropriate stopping technique quickly.

The techniques of bringing the ball under control quickly must be mastered to as high a level as possible. Accuracy in passing demands care in looking for passing possibilities and striking the ball. To take care demands a fractionally increased amount of time. The player who cannot control the ball and cause it to drop dead at his feet rarely has the time in which he can afford to take trouble over his passing. He is always hurried because bringing the ball under control takes so long. Another, and equally important application of stopping techniques, involves controlling the ball while moving or turning away from an opponent. If a player attempts to trap a ball towards an opponent, he is offering that opponent an opportunity to tackle and, at the same time, he is reducing the amount of time available for making an accurate pass. In football, space is time and the more space a player makes for himself the greater the amount of time in which he can play and take care over the application of his techniques.

GOALKEEPING

We have seen that the basic techniques of stopping the ball are exactly the same for a goalkeeper as for any other player, the only difference being that the goalkeeper has the added advantage of being able to use his hands. Generally speaking the following principles apply:

1. His body should be behind the ball whenever possible.
2. He should always use both hands to catch the ball or to make a save, whenever he can.
3. As he catches the ball he should relax and withdraw his body, his hands, or both to absorb the force of the shot.
4. He should keep his eyes behind the flight of the ball for as long as possible. Some goalkeepers experience difficulty in catching a ball which is travelling at head height because they move their head just before they catch it. This may be caused by trying to catch and move away at the same time. Alternatively it may be that the goalkeeper is looking for a passing opportunity or for an opponent's challenge.

Catching the ball cleanly is the most important of these factors. Having established control by catching the ball the goalkeeper is in a position of almost unassailable authority. Any player who is apprehensive about the possibility of challenge while he is trying to stop, catch, or control the ball will make frequent mistakes.

CATCHING OR FIELDING THE BALL

A goalkeeper is required to catch or field the ball at all heights from ground level to a height which requires a full upward or sideways leap. Wherever possible his hands will be slightly behind the ball as it arrives and, as quickly as possible, the ball will be pulled into the pit of his stomach when it has been caught, particularly when there is the possibility of an immediate challenge.

Plate 34

1. For low shots where playing conditions are difficult or where the shot is a fairly hard one, the goalkeeper turns both his feet sideways to the direction of the shot and bends down on one knee. His upper body is twisted full face towards the oncoming ball and his hands are at ground level, palms upwards waiting to channel the ball into his stomach. This bending position, with no gaps between his knees, presents the biggest possible stopping surface to the ball and the goal-keeper's eyes are close to the ball's line of flight. The elbows are always tucked well in and parallel to each other to prevent any chance of the ball escaping (*plate* 34). This kneeling position allows the keeper to collect the ball and move away fairly quickly. Any kneeling position in which the knees are towards the ball should be avoided. These positions can result in the ball bouncing away from the goalkeeper's control.

2. To field balls which are above ground level but which are not chest high, most goalkeepers stand erect with legs together and straight and, if necessary, they bend forward from the hips to prepare the channel into which the ball will travel (*plate* 36).

3. For balls which approach at chest height or above the goalkeeper stands erect but slightly crouched. His hands are raised towards the ball, with the palms pointing in the same direction. The ball is caught using the so-called baseball catch (*plate* 35).

Plate 35   **Plate 36**

<table>
<tr><td>**Plate 37**</td><td>**Plate 38**</td></tr>
</table>

Any inclination to push the ball and knock it down must be avoided. Good goalkeepers can catch and hold the ball in almost any circumstances. Tipping the ball over the bar or around the upright and punching the ball away are occasionally necessary. They may look more spectacular but the goalkeeper most respected by forwards is the one who is an expert catcher. Where a goalkeeper can move to deal with a shot or a cross he should move towards the ball. This gives him the advantage of getting to it early, and a forward movement allows him to jump higher and more effectively off his best jumping foot. Whenever there is the likelihood of having to go for the ball a goalkeeper should be moving on his feet in some way or other however slightly; in doing so he has overcome the inertia of his body weight and the resultant spring, run or jump will be quicker and higher.

TIPPING OR PALMING THE BALL OVER THE BAR
OR AROUND THE UPRIGHT

Most goalkeepers prefer to use that part of the palm of the hand nearest to and including the fingers. This allows the palming movement to be carried out with the least possibility of error. The fist

Plate 39

Plate 40

Plate 41

Plate 42

Plate 43

is occasionally used but because of its shape when clenched the fist can cause errors to occur. When pushing a cross or a corner-kick over the bar goalkeepers tend to use the hand and arm which is nearest to the field of play since this gives a greater freedom of arm swing but it is difficult to lay down rules. The goalkeeper has to use many variations of basic techniques (*plates* 37 *and* 38).

PUNCHING

Whenever possible a goalkeeper should use both fists together (*plates* 39 *and* 40). This makes for a bigger and flatter punching surface and the contact which results is safer and more accurate. Occasionally, however, and particularly when dealing with high crosses, he has to punch the ball away with one hand. Most goal-keepers use the hand furthest from the direction in which they intend the ball to go (*plates* 41, 42 *and* 43). This is usually upfield or away from goal towards the wings. The punch is thus a natural overarm swing in the direction required.

JUMPING TO CATCH OR PUNCH THE BALL

We have already seen how the one-footed take off makes for the greatest height and how any small preliminary movement assists

225

the height and speed of the jump itself. When a goalkeeper jumps to punch or catch the ball, he often does so in the middle or towards the middle of a group of players, all of whom may be trying to jump to head the ball. There is obviously the possibility of collisions either in the air or after landing and goalkeepers must protect themselves whenever possible. Most goalkeepers avoid showing the fully stretched frontal part of the body when jumping by lifting the non jumping leg, bent, across the body. This, of course, will be the leg nearest to adjacent players. Some goalkeepers raise both knees as protection but this technique causes problems if he is knocked off balance while in the air. When tucking the body completely in this way the goalkeeper is increasing any tendency for his body to turn or spin. Any contact with adjacent players is likely to cause this spin to be increased which means that a safe landing will be difficult, particularly while continuing to hold the ball.

NARROWING SHOOTING ANGLES AND SMOTHERING THE BALL

All goalkeepers should understand the functions of all their defenders and they must be equally capable of reading the developments of opposing attacking movements. The goalkeeper who stays on the goal-line all the time is giving away his great advantage within the whole of the penalty-area—permission to use his hands. As he develops experience in anticipating through passes he can cut off many dangerous passing movements on the edge of his own penalty-area and occasionally, outside it. There is nothing more frustrating for a forward line to find carefully judged passes past the centre half or inside the full back being safely gathered by an intelligent goalkeeper on the edge of his penalty-area. Many goalkeepers patrol the front of the penalty-area, moving across it and changing position as the direction of an opposing attack changes. At the same time they may retreat to within the goal area if play is developing in across the field movements. In doing this goalkeepers calculate the risk by calculating the ability of the opposition to produce a surprise high shot. Goalkeepers are, for long periods, observers only and this enables them to gain and retain a great deal of knowledge about opposing players' techniques and skills.

When an opposing player is in a shooting position the goalkeeper's main job is to present his opponent with the smallest possible target. In a frontal position where the goalkeeper is standing in the centre of his goal on the goal line the largest possible target is presented (*plate* 44). As the goalkeeper moves forward

Plate 44

Plate 45

towards his opponent, the frontal area of the target is reduced (*plate* 45). If the opposing forward approaches goal from an angle the target is also reduced and if, as in the previous example, the goalkeeper advances towards the forward he can block his view of the goal almost entirely. Once again the goalkeeper calculates the risk involved as follows:

1. If he does not advance the forward has the greatest target area at which to aim.
2. If he advances too far too soon, the forward who has the ball may pass to another player.
3. If he advances too far, the forward may attempt to chip or lob the shot over his head. The further he advances the easier this becomes.
4. If he advances too quickly and without control and balance he makes it easy for the forward to dribble the ball round him and into goal.
5. If the forward is running very quickly his control over the ball may not be so good. In this situation a quick advance by the goalkeeper may enable him to fall on the ball before the forward can regain control.

As is the case with all defenders, good goalkeepers will try to 'jockey' a forward, who is bearing down on goal, into the least dangerous position. If the goalkeeper knows that the forward is right-footed, he will advance in such a way as to try to force him to move left, that is to say, into a position where the forward has to try a shot with his weaker foot. The goalkeeper may also feint to rush forward and instead move back, trying to slow the forward down and trying to make him change his mind. This may give time for other defenders to recover and make a challenge.

FALLING ON THE BALL OR SMOTHERING A SHOT

Assuming that the approaching forward is moving towards goal at an angle (most forwards prefer an angled approach to enable them to use their better-shooting foot) the goalkeeper will go down with his body behind the ball in a sideways position (*plates* 46 *and* 47). Whether the upper body, and therefore the hands, are to the left or the right will depend on the direction in which he anticipates the forward will shoot or dribble the ball. The goalkeeper is trying to produce the largest and longest wall possible behind the ball (*plate* 48). As he grasps the ball and pulls it into his body, he rolls over towards his opponent and folds his head, arms and knees in

Plate 46

Plate 47

Plate 48

Plate 49

towards his stomach to protect the ball and to protect himself (*plate* 49). Inexperienced goalkeepers often make a late decision to dive for the ball at an opponent's feet and, being late, find that they have to dive forwards. This means that they are leading with a largely unprotected head and the possibility of sustaining an injury is increased.

EVADING A CHALLENGE

The goalkeeper has a considerable advantage in being able to control the ball with his hands. He is not, however, protected completely from a challenger. He may be charged when holding the ball or if he attempts to obstruct an opponent or when he has moved outside the goal area. The extent to which he can move freely when in possession of the ball is governed by the fact that he cannot take more than four steps without bouncing the ball. When catching the ball the goalkeeper must be prepared for a challenge. He must dodge and feint while bouncing the ball. Most goalkeepers bounce the ball with one hand and catch the rebound with two. Whatever basic practices a goalkeeper may employ, it is always useful and realistic to challenge him. A player should be nearby to challenge for the ball should it be dropped or mis-fielded. He must develop a high degree of concentration since a goalkeeper's mistakes are usually final.

CLEARING THE BALL

Having gained possession of the ball a goalkeeper is in a position to start an attack. He must be as accurate as any player on the field with kicks and throws. Too often goalkeepers kick the ball high in the air and far upfield in the belief that the farther the safer. If he gives possession to the opposition the goalkeeper will find that he is back where he started, saving another shot, sooner rather than later. He should master most basic passing techniques since he will have to push a quick pass to a waiting colleague outside the penalty-area, kick a long pass off the ground and on the volley (out of his hands) or low drive a half volley twenty or thirty yards. If he is two footed so much the better.

THROWING THE BALL

A thrown ball is usually an accurate pass. Such a pass can be given by rolling the ball underarm as in bowls or throwing it overarm. If such a pass is on the ground it will be easier to control by the

Plate 50

Plate 51

player who receives it. Where possible, therefore, a goalkeeper should use the cricket ball or javelin throwing technique (*plates 50 and* 51). The longer the throw the longer the time taken by the goalkeeper to prepare himself for it and the longer the time for opponents to move and anticipate it. Short accurate throws given quickly are better than long, inaccurate throws given slowly.

GOALKEEPING PRACTICES

In threes, one ball between two; the various methods of catching and fielding a ball can be practised as follows:

1. A serves to B in such a way as to demand a certain type of catch. Having served, A runs to challenge B who must catch the ball, immediately evade the challenge and, as quickly as possible, give a pass either by throwing or kicking to C. C stands at varying distances outside the penalty-area or away from B's position. Occasionally, when practising a particular goalkeeping technique, A will try to surprise B with a different service. Practice must never be automatic and mechanical.

2. A fourth player can be introduced to mark C. This player will test the accuracy and control of the goalkeeper's passing. If it is a bad clearance he will be able to intercept the ball or make an immediate challenge on C, the receiver.

   Whenever and wherever possible, skill practices must take place in a real goalmouth. A goalkeeper's skill involves an ability to know where he is relative to the goal behind him and relative to the goalmouth and penalty-area. He must become accustomed to judging his position by using the various field markings as a guide.

3. Two players, A and B, approach the penalty-area interpassing over a distance of ten to fifteen yards. As A and B interpass the goalkeeper adjusts his position to cover the possibility of a shot. The shot is made from outside the penalty-area. Occasionally the two attacking players will continue into the penalty-area and one of them will try to dribble the ball round the goalkeeper or alternatively to chip the ball over the goalkeeper's head. This practice can be made more realistic by the inclusion of a defender who is allowed to challenge the two attackers as they enter the penalty-area, or cover the goal behind the goalkeeper as he advances to narrow the angle for the approaching forwards.

233

2. Quick change of position to deal with rapidly changing method of attack is important to a goalkeeper. In *fig.* 139, A approaches the goal well down the wing and crosses the ball towards goal. B is another attacker who, if opportunity occurs, can attempt a shot on goal. The goalkeeper, X, will deal with the cross or a shot while being covered by another

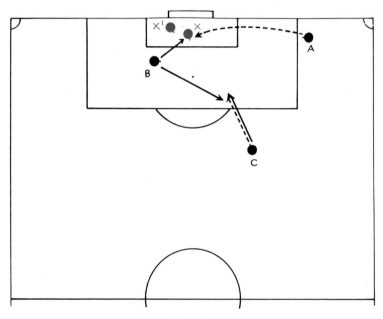

Fig. 139

defender X[1] on the goal line. When the first practice situation has been concluded player C approaches goal and, toghether with B, they will manoeuvre for a quick shot at goal. Defender X[1] can either challenge the attackers or cover his goalkeeper.

3. Working on both sides of an un-netted goal or an artificial goal made by using corner flags, A and B shoot at goal from varying distances, at different angles and using different techniques. While the goalkeeper is dealing with a shot from A, B will have altered his position. As soon as the goalkeeper has dealt with one attempt on goal he must turn around and adjust his position to deal with the threat from behind him.

4. As we have seen, a goalkeeper must know how far from goal he can safely advance, bearing in mind the possibility of a

long lobbed shot by an attacker. This can be calculated roughly in practice as follows: the goalkeeper positions himself a certain distance from goal. An attacker who is also a certain distance from the penalty-area approaches the ball to try to lob a shot over the goalkeeper's head into goal. As soon as the attacker moves towards the ball, the goalkeeper runs back to his goal-line to try to make the required save. By altering the position of the attacker and allowing the goalkeeper to adjust his position relative to the goal it should be possible for a goalkeeper to work out the position in the penalty area which will allow him to narrow the approaching and shooting angles of an oncoming forward and still, if the situation changes, recover to his goal-line position in time.

5. In *fig.* 140 three central attackers, A, B, and C, are positioned among two central defenders (X) some distance outside the

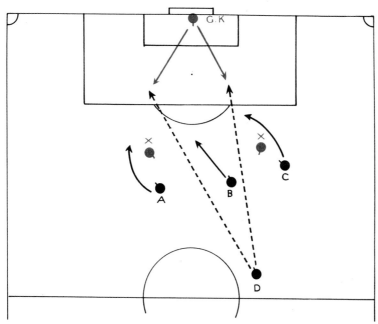

Fig. 140

penalty-area. Server D tries to pass the ball through the defenders, round them, or over them so that the ball is collected by an attacker somewhere inside the penalty-area. The goalkeeper attempts to read the passing possibilities and to

235

intercept the pass towards the edge of his penalty-area. He must remain aware of the possibility of a surprise long shot. The server is free to try a long shot if the goalkeeper advances too far too soon. Occasionally the server may advance with the ball himself and attacking play will develop quite freely to test the goalkeeper's reaction to unfamiliar situations.

6. In *fig.* 141 the ball is lobbed into the goalmouth towards the edge of the goal area. The goalkeeper jumps to catch or to punch clear according to the challenge of one, two or three attackers (A, B, and C). As the practice develops the ball will

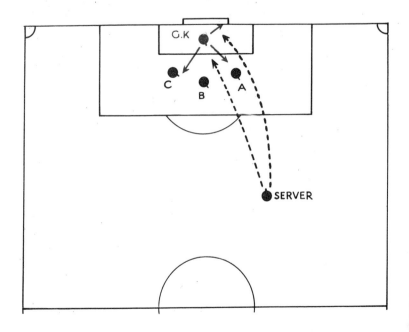

Figure 141

occasionally be served beyond the central group of players, or, alternatively, towards the goal. This requires that the goalkeeper must allow for the possibility of swerve in the cross-kick by waiting until the last possible moment before moving to the edge of his goal area.

7. Great goalkeepers are able to dominate not only the goal area but also a considerable part of the penalty-area, particularly from long cross-kicks or corners. This skill is not merely a

236

matter of moving out quickly; it includes the ability to avoid a number of attackers and defenders who may be inside the penalty-area. The maximum distance which a goalkeeper can safely cover and still jump to save can only be found by trial and error. Goalkeepers must practise these skills in situations as close as possible to the actual game. Where possible, they must have constant practice at saving shots or collecting the ball when their view of the ball and their freedom of movement is restricted or hampered by other opposing and defending players. It is also important that, having made a save, the goalkeeper should be required to control the ball against a challenge and, as quickly as he can, make an accurate clearance by kicking or throwing to a target man. As with other players, a goalkeeper's skill involves making the correct decision when faced with a number of alternatives. When coaching for an improvement in skill these alternatives, to a greater or a lesser extent, must always be present.

DRIBBLING

The most notable developments of modern soccer are those evident in systems of play and tactics. The organization of team play is at a much higher level than in the past and, in consequence, a great deal of thought is given to the most efficient use of individuals. Some deplore this accent upon organization, claiming that it destroys individual ability and the flair which great individuals have brought to the game in the past. Spectators enjoy the game for different reasons, but the evolution of the game makes it inevitable that organized team play will develop even further. Soccer is a team game and efficiency must come from a greater study of its many constituent parts. This happens in all great national games, particularly when a fully professional approach by clubs, players, coaches, and managers is involved.

From time to time, in the nature of things, defensive organization will dominate the game. These periods will be followed by new and exciting attacking cycles in the pattern of change. The advent of the stopper centre-half, following the change in the offside law in 1925, was assumed to herald the death of attacking play. The stopper centre-half was offset by twin centre-forwards. These, in turn, were countered by the development of double centre-half play and subsequently the sweeper centre-back. We are now using defensive players as surprise attackers and, no doubt, future developments in attacking play will see a reversion to attacking centre-halves and systems calling for considerable interchange between attacking players and defenders.

But whatever the form of organization, the individual player will always be of paramount importance. However well organized a defence may be, the ability of one opposing player to beat one or more defenders by holding the ball and dribbling will always cause marked defensive problems. All players, irrespective of their positions, must have this ability and must be encouraged to develop the skill as much as individual differences will allow. Not everyone will become a Stanley Matthews but everyone can acquire some level of skill at dribbling. This belief is in no way revolutionary since most people first develop an interest in the game through dribbling a ball. Without trying to establish an order of priority for learning the techniques of football, it can be said that shooting and dribbling should rank high on such an order.

Dribbling is when a player keeps the ball and attempts to take it past one or more opponents. The different ways in which this can be attempted are limitless but there are principles which must be understood:

1. Generally speaking a good dribbler of the ball always keeps the ball within comfortable playing distance. This distance will be determined by the ease with which he can move the ball in any direction through a full circle and remain within playing distance of it.

2. The player should be in an evenly balanced position in order that he can move in any direction. This particularly applies where he is waiting for a defender to make the first move.

3. The player should try to make his opponent move into an off balance position. This is the equivalent to dodging in that a person pretends to move in one direction when he intends to move in another. He does this by various movements of his feet and body aimed at causing his opponent to react and block his path of travel.

Early practices might involve a group of players, having a ball each, dribbling freely within a certain area such as the penalty-area. The emphasis in this technique which is, in fact, running and dodging with the ball, will be as follows: control the ball while looking away; the player does not concentrate his attention on the ball but 'splits' it between the ball and players nearby who might run into him or interfere in some way with the free passage around the area.

We might then set small problems such as:

1. Look for a space and dribble into it as quickly as possible.
2. Left foot only—right foot only.
3. Half the players must travel clockwise and half anti-clockwise.
4. On a signal, stop with your foot on the ball, pull it back, and move off in the opposite direction.
5. Frequent stops followed by a quick dribble into a free space.

Plate 52

The technique of 'looking away' while dribbling is of major importance and players should develop a feel for the control of the ball rather than finding themselves looking at it all the time (*plate* 52). As the players' ability increases so the size of the area can be reduced. This means that their control must be greater and their awareness of other players more acute.

The next activity might be concerned with the principle of throwing an opponent off balance. The players work in pairs and they stand on opposite sides of a white line which is perhaps ten yards long. At each end there can be a circle one foot in diameter. Neither player is ever allowed to cross the line and the one with the ball attempts to dribble it into either of the two circles. His opponent tries to stay in front of him all the time (*fig.* 142).

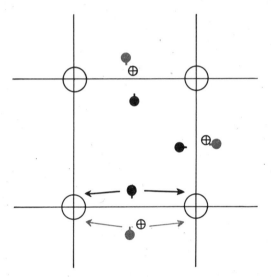

Figure 142

As the player with the ball attempts to put the ball into one of the circles his opponent will attempt to put one foot in the circle first. This means that the player with the ball must start again. Faced with this problem the player with the ball will immediately begin to try methods of dodging and feinting which are natural to him. At first he will dodge and run with the ball at a tremendous pace. This is the time at which the coach will emphasize the importance of change of pace in deceiving an opponent. The player will realize that a change of pace from very slow to quick is more easily achieved and far less demanding than a change of pace from quick to quicker. The player learns to wait for the moment when his opponent is really off balance. The same practice can continue where the player with the ball has his back towards his opponent. He then has to develop an awareness of what is happening without being able to see his opponent's reactions clearly. The target will be the same. The coach can then introduce various feinting and ball manipulating techniques as he sees a need for them. They will be introduced as possibilities but they will not be forced upon the players. These might include:

1. Feinting to play the ball by passing a foot over the ball (*plate* 53).
2. Dragging the ball along with one foot and stopping it with the other.
3. Feinting with the shoulders.
4. Playing the ball quickly backwards and forwards from one foot to the other.

Plate 53

Plate 54

The last practice situation, where a player dodges sideways with his back towards his opponent, leads to another important principle of dribbling. This involves screening the ball from an opponent's view.

SCREENING (*plate* 54)

A player is screening the ball when he places his body between his opponent and the ball while keeping it within playing distance.

A player may have attempted to dribble past an opponent face to face and failed. The next time he might use a screening technique in order to make tackling by his opponent rather more difficult. Alternatively he might screen his opponent from the ball while holding it and waiting for team mates to move into supporting positions for a pass (*plates* 55, 56, and 57). Using one ball between two players, where one screens the ball from his opponent, touch targets might be set for the player with the ball. He might be asked to try to touch the ball twenty, thirty or forty times before his opponent can take it away from him. The opponent tries as hard as possible to take the ball away from the player with the ball. They might be asked to perform this practice in an area ten yards by sixty yards square. Further progression might involve starting

Plate 55

Plate 56

Plate 57

in the screening position whereby the player with the ball attempts to get past his opponent by alternating between screening and dribbling. For adult players, one against one, on a pitch perhaps fifteen yards by eight yards with goals at each end, is excellent for practising dribbling and, at the same time, it is extremely hard work. In order to restrict shooting, there is a semi-circle in front of each goal with a radius of perhaps two to three yards. Before a player can shoot he must dribble into this shooting zone. In this game, the only possibility for a player to rest is when he can screen the ball effectively.

'SHOWING THE BALL'

'Showing the ball' involves one player deliberately encouraging an opponent to challenge or tackle for the ball by making him think that the player in possession cannot control it effectively. This can be achieved by pushing the ball towards him and perhaps drawing it away. Working once again in a small area we might start the practice off by setting the player with the ball the problem of escaping with it from a corner. Initially his opponent might be three or four yards away. As dribbling skill increases so the starting distance between dribbler and opponent is reduced. An important technique when showing an opponent the ball is con-

244

trolling the ball with the sole of the foot. This enables a feint to be made at the ball while letting it apparently, roll out of reach.

RUNNING AT AN OPPONENT

One of the methods which an experienced defender will use against a clever dribbler will be to retreat, particularly when he knows his opponent to be clever and quick. He retreats in order to be already moving in the direction in which he knows his opponent will move and also to join up with his other defenders. Furthermore, the intelligent defender will try to jockey his opponent into a small space where his opponent is restricted perhaps by the touch-line, the goal-line or both. An important technique, therefore, involves committing a defender by moving towards him without reducing speed. A retreating defender usually causes an attacker to slow down and attackers must be aware of this. The ability to dribble at speed towards a retreating opponent and then to beat him, perhaps by increasing speed, requires considerable practice. Too often clever dribblers allow defenders to dictate to them. This is good defensive play but the player with the ball must be aware of it and prevent the defender from dominating the situation. For a defender, who is faced by a player in possession of the ball, there is a considerable problem presented when the player with the ball moves towards him rather than, as is more often the case, away from him. The defender cannot allow the attacker to move towards him indefinitely. Sooner or later he must *do* something, which is what the player with the ball should be waiting for. Changing direction at speed is a difficult but important dribbling technique.

It is interesting to study what happens to a defender as he is made to change his balance when an opponent dribbles the ball towards him. A player who is evenly balanced over both feet is in a good position to move quickly in any direction. Before a player can move, however, he usually shifts his weight slightly away from the direction in which he intends to move in order to start the push off in the required direction. At this moment, when his weight has been transferred, it is almost impossible for him to move in the same direction. In order to do so he has to shift the weight to the opposite side, once again in order to be able to push off. When a clever player beats an opponent in a dribble he does it one of two ways. In the first he causes his opponent to overbalance to such an extent that the defender is incapable of moving in any direction. In these circumstances the player with the ball beats his opponent by passing him on the side opposite to that in which the defender is leaning. In the second he feints to go one way and then moves in the same direction. The defender reacts by pushing in the direction of the feint, commits his weight to that side of his body. The second movement finds him with his weight on the wrong foot.

Close observation of any good dribbler will show him making continuous attempts to throw his opponent off balance. Some, like Stanley Matthews, do this by tapping the ball from one foot to another. They are tempting the defender into a tackle or causing him to continually transfer his weight from one foot to the other. Others employ twisting movements of the hips and shoulders to give an opponent the impression that they are about to pass rather than dribble past him. Others make elaborate feint plays at the ball, past it, or over it. All are attempting to unbalance the defender.

SELLING A DUMMY

This involves the essence of dribbling which is to create a false impression in an opponent's mind. It can be achieved by feinting and dodging as we have already seen, and it can be greatly assisted by using a nearby team mate as a decoy. If a defender, faced by an opponent with the ball, is aware that another opposing player is nearby, perhaps available for a pass, he must bear this passing possibility in mind when challenging the player with the ball, particularly if he knows that this second opponent is nearer to goal than the man with the ball. The defender will try to position himself to intercept the pass and to stop the dribble. The player with the ball may position his body as if preparing to pass but at the last moment he will swerve away around the defender. Even if no team mate is nearby a clever dribbler will often deliberately look past the defender and prepare to give a pass as if one were there. He uses an imaginary opponent to create doubt in the defender's mind.

In running past an opponent with the ball many different techniques can be used. Some defenders, in concentrating on anticipating an opponent's dribbling movement, stand with their legs wide open. It may be possible to play the ball through the defender's legs while running past him. When watching Pelé, the great Brazilian player, dribbling it often seems that he tries to play the ball against an opponent's legs before moving on to collect the rebound. Similarly it is possible to push the ball past an opponent while running around and past him on the opposite side. These techniques demand a high degree of quickness in dribbling. This ability to move very quickly over ten or fifteen yards, frequently from a standing position, is very important in developing dribbling skill.

Thoughtful positional play and an intelligent service of the ball from his team mates can greatly assist even the cleverest dribbler. We have seen how a supporting player can help the player with the ball to put an opposing defender in two minds. It is important that supporting players do not obstruct him when he is trying to

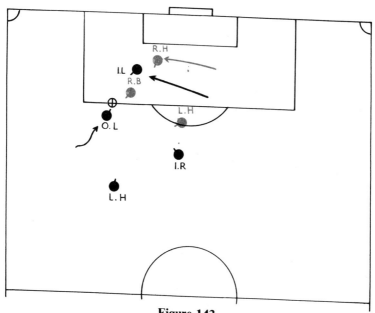

Figure 143

beat his opponent. In *fig.* 143 the outside-left is in a good position to attack the opposing full-back. If he is successful he will probably move into the penalty-area, perhaps aiming to reach the goal-line, from which he can make an effective pass back or a cross to the other forwards. The winger is well supported by his inside-right and, from behind, by the left half-back, but the inside-left has moved behind the opposing full-back and the defending right-half has shadowed this movement. In doing this the inside-left has reduced the space in which the outside-left can attack the opposing right-back.

In *fig.* 144 the inside-right is still supporting the outside-left but has moved into a deeper supporting position. He is trying to tempt the opposing left-half away from a covering position on the right-back. In the same way the inside-left has moved into the inside-right position taking the opposing wing-half (RH) away from the area near the ball. It is now possible for the outside-left to attack the opposing right-back since space has been created into which he can move if the dribbling movement is successful.

Wherever a clever dribbler is most effective, and this usually means near the opposing penalty-area, his colleagues, who should know how he prefers to use his dribbling technique, should always try to draw as many defenders as possible away from covering positions. This question of the most valuable area of the field in

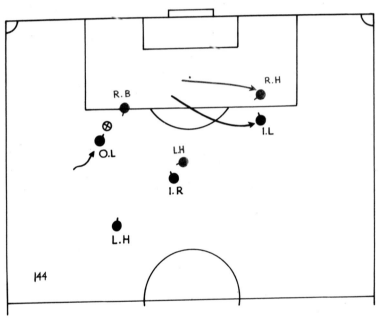

Figure 144

which to use dribbling skill is most important. Too often we see clever players displaying all their tricks in their own half or in mid-field. Experienced defenders watch this display with interest and remember what they see. The clever player then wonders why opposing defenders are more successful in dealing with the problems which he tries to present near to the opposing goal.

The service of passes to the player who is deceptive with the ball is also important. Some players prefer to receive passes which allow them to collect the ball at speed. These are the aggressive dribblers who prefer to force a defender into error by moving towards him fairly quickly. Others prefer to receive the ball at their feet and, having received and controlled it, to take their time in tempting a defender to make a challenge. Some prefer to receive the ball when they have drawn a defender into a fairly close marking position and others require a large space in which they can take their time in creating doubts and uncertainty in an opponent's mind. There are clever dribblers who are strong and fast runners and who prefer passes to be played past defenders. Others are quick over short distances but who are not strong and persistent runners over distances greater than ten to fifteen yards. In order to bring out the best of each individual's ability he should receive the passing service which he prefers. Part of the attraction of soccer is that different individuals can contribute effectively in different ways. An individual's strengths in skill and technique are more important than his weaknesses.

Running with the ball will play a part in various fitness training methods. During this sort of practice most players indulge in 'shadow' dribbling against imaginary opponents. The true skill of dribbling can only be developed against active opponents. In creating effective practice situations, other than those of a general nature which have already been mentioned, a coach must think of the parts of the field and the exact match circumstances in which a player's dribbling skill is most often required.

Examples, for the various team positions, might be as follows:

Wingers

1. (1 *v* 1) The winger is given the ball near to the corner-flag and he must attempt to get out of this position and pass into the penalty-area. As the winger improves, the space in which he works is reduced and we may introduce a covering half-back as an additional obstacle. Initially this half-back would be required to station himself ten or fifteen yards behind his full-back. As a further step in the progression an inside-forward could be introduced to support the winger and, obviously, this player would affect the positioning of the covering wing-half-back.

2. The winger, in possession of the ball, runs at the full-back from a position perhaps twenty yards outside the penalty-area. The full-back can only retreat to the edge of the penalty-area at which stage he must challenge. As in (1) this practice can be elaborated by adding more players. In this case we might introduce the supporting inside-forward first thus confronting the full-back with a 2 *v* 1 choice and creating the possibility for the winger to use the inside-forward as a decoy.

As the winger's ability improves so an additional defender would be introduced.

Centre-forwards

1. The ball is served up to the centre-forward from a distance of forty yards or so. The centre-forward is covered by a centre-half who himself is covered by another central defender. Having received the ball the centre-forward attempts to retain possession until one or two supporting players arrive from thirty to forty yards away. Here he will have to use screening skill to hold possession although if he can draw one defender away from the other he will be encouraged to try to beat him by screening and turning. This practice will result in a 2 *v* 2 or 3 *v* 2 situation in which the attackers will try to score against the defenders. We can emphasize the use of dribbling by restricting the retreat of defenders to the edge of the penalty-area.

2. The centre-forward is on the edge of the penalty-area covered by a defender who, initially, is stationed five or six yards nearer to goal. The ball is served to the centre-forward who attempts to manoeuvre into position for a shot at goal. He cannot shoot until he is actually inside the penalty-area. Additional players are introduced as the practice develops.

Inside-forwards

1. The inside-forward begins running with the ball some distance from goal. He is faced by a full-back and has a winger outside him. The inside-forward attempts to run towards the inside of the full-back by feinting to make a pass to the winger. The full-back faced with this 2 *v* 1 situation will jockey the inside-forward to try to make him pass the ball. Later the winger and the inside-forward will be encouraged to interchange and to use each other as decoys to beat their opponent using dribbling techniques.

2. The inside-forward takes the ball inside the penalty-area. He is fairly closely marked by three defenders. When the practice begins he tries to hold the ball and dribble himself into a shooting position while staying in the penalty-area. Another forward will then be added to extend the possibilities open to him.

Wing-half-backs

1. The wing-half-back will play the ball up to an inside-forward who is marked by a defender. The inside-forward plays a return pass back to the wing-half who attempts to burst past the defender for a shot at goal.

COACHING AND TEACHING TECHNIQUES

2. The ball is thrown out by the goalkeeper to the wing-half-back who receives it facing the goalkeeper. The half-back is challenged by an opponent from behind. He must screen the ball and attempt to beat his opponent. While screening the ball he can play the ball back to the goalkeeper. Later two opponents challenge the wing-half-back who then can be given another problem by the introduction of an inside-forward who must come into support from a position near the centre circle.

Centre-half-backs

1. A full-back and his opposing winger are stationed about forty yards from goal. The ball is served over or inside the full-back for the winger to run on to. From his normal central position the centre-half must move across the field, intercept the ball and try to beat the oncoming wing man. The possibility of a decoy play exists if the centre-half decides to use the full-back to assist him in the dribbling movement.

2. The centre-half receives the ball in the centre of the field and he is immediately challenged by the opposing centre-forward. He must try to dribble the ball around the challenger and play a pass to a nearby wing-half. We can also give him the additional problem of screening and holding the ball and perhaps playing a pass back to the goalkeeper. Again the introduction of additional players will make the practice even more realistic.

Full-backs

1. A winger covered by a full-back moves infield with the ball to create space between himself and the touch-line. His own full-back runs into this space and, as he runs past the winger, the ball is passed to him. The full-back, now operating as an attacker, must attempt to cross the ball from the opposing goal-line or cut in and shoot while being challenged by a covering wing-half.

2. The full-back receives the ball out towards the touch-line and moving towards his own goal while being closely shadowed by an opposing winger. His own winger can attempt to move into a supporting position and the full-back must attempt to screen the ball away from the challenging wing and ultimately beat him by dribbling or interpassing with the supporting wing.

These, and other practices, are developed by using imagination to devise realistic situations which actually occur in the game. These situations are then simplified to their basic components and gradually re-developed as a player's skill increases. All such practice situations must compel a player to make a decision related to actual playing circumstances. It follows that a reasonable freedom of choice must also be available to him.

TACKLING

Tackling is one of two techniques which produce difficulties for both teacher and coach. The other is heading. Even a slightly incorrect technique can bring about a painful experience. Probably, most poor tacklers had some painful experience of tackling as very young players. Alternatively it may be that where a young player has developed a high level of dribbling skill his early experience has been entirely concerned with evading tackles rather than making them. Nevertheless, tackling is a vital part of the modern player's skill since, increasingly, the division of responsibility between so-called attackers and defenders is decreasing. In the modern game, with its demands for interchange of positions, forwards are required to become efficient defenders and defenders are required to be effective in attacking play.

Different tackling techniques tend to be more common in different phases of the game. The front block tackle is most commonly used by half-backs since they frequently tackle players who are approaching them face to face. The side block tackle is often used by forwards, particularly inside-forwards, who may be required to chase an opponent in possession of the ball. The sliding tackle is most frequently used by full-backs since they are usually stationed near the touch-lines; the sliding tackle is a desperate measure usually resulting in the ball being kicked out of play. However, all players can and should be familiar with all tackling techniques. There is nothing worse than for a full-back, who has gained possession of the ball, to find that he is being persistently challenged by a determined winger. When possession of the ball has been lost all players have a duty to make it difficult for their opponents to retain possession and, where possible, to challenge for the ball by tackling.

THE FRONT BLOCK TACKLE

In all situations where one player intends to tackle another, the tackler should attempt to manoeuvre his opponent into a position where:
1. The least possible danger will arise if the tackle fails.
2. The space in which the player with the ball can dodge, turn, or avoid the tackle is as small as possible.

3. Other defending players are available to cover him.
4. He (the tackler) can decide when the timing advantage is on his side. The player with the ball will try to tempt his opponent to tackle when the timing advantage is on his side, of course.

All players have certain strengths and weaknesses and these should be studied. For example, most players prefer to use one foot when controlling the ball. Even good two-footed players show this preference and the more difficult the situation the more they will use the foot in which they have the greatest confidence. If the tackler can jockey his opponent in the direction of the opponent's weaker foot he will be in the best position to tackle effectively. In the case of a player who is right-footed we would try to make him move to his left and vice versa. While his controlling movements are being made with his 'good' foot he is being forced in a direction in which, sooner or later, he may be compelled to use his 'bad' foot. Close observation of players will also reveal their inclination towards certain types of feinting movements. These are usually developed, almost as habits, to enable a player to move in the direction in which he wants to go. Great players, of course, can move in any direction with equal facility but even these have a liking for a certain direction and a certain foot.

Jockeying is an important skill in as much as it is an attempt to take the advantage away from the player with the ball. In the same way, feinting movements are used to try to make the player with

Plate 58

the ball change his mind. Good tacklers are patient enough to wait for the timing advantage to be on their side. This is particularly the case when an opponent has established control over the ball. It is often possible, however, to make a challenge as an opponent prepares to receive the ball. In these circumstances there is considerable advantage to the tackler because the receiver of the ball has two problems, controlling the pass, and evading the tackle. Added to which, of course, is the possibility of the tackler arriving to make a challenge early enough to intercept the ball.

As with other techniques there are certain basic principles which apply to all block tackles (*plate* 58).

1. The tackle is timed to coincide with the opponent attempting to play the ball.
2. The force of the tackling foot is applied through the centre of the ball.
3. The non tackling foot is placed to one side of and behind the ball.
4. As contact is made the full weight of the body is transferred onto the standing foot and the tackling foot which, by this time, is blocking the ball against the opponent's feet.

The block tackle is made with the inside of the foot since this provides the largest possible blocking surface. Both knees are slightly bent to absorb the shock of the tackling impact and also to lower the centre of gravity of the tackler. This ensures that he is in a position in which he will be difficult to overbalance, particularly if a shoulder charge is attempted at the same time as the tackle. This is why short players have an advantage over tall players in a tackling situation and why short, and perhaps stocky, players are often the strongest and most tenacious tacklers. Having caused the ball to be wedged between his foot and his opponent's the tackler will maintain a firm pressure against the ball while leaning into it. At this stage one or the other of the players will attempt to gain possession of the ball in the following ways:

(*a*) By lifting or rolling the ball over his opponent's foot (*plate* 59).
(*b*) By dragging the ball out of the tackle sideways.
(*c*) By forcing the ball between his opponent's feet (*plate* 60).
(*d*) By shoulder charging in such a way as to cause his opponent to overbalance.

Strong tacklers will perhaps wait fractionally for their opponent to try to change the application of force against the ball and then use this momentary release of force to gain possession themselves.

| Plate 59 | Plate 60 |

Common faults in front block tackling

1. The tackler lunges at the ball when his opponent is well balanced and slightly out of distance. This places his opponent at an advantage since the tackler cannot apply controlled force against the ball. Depending on his distance away from the ball the tackling leg is straight and his weight is entirely committed onto one foot. This means that the tackler cannot adjust his position and that he cannot recover should the player with the ball resist or evade the tackle successfully. In this position the tackler leaves himself open to injury since a straight tackling leg always creates the possibility of a broken tackling leg, particularly when that leg is stretched forward.

2. The tackler goes into the tackle half-heartedly. When one or the other of the two players 'feels' for the tackle he has to take all the shock of impact. Where both go into the tackle firmly the ball takes most of this shock. This can be proven by wedging a ball firmly with either the sole or the inside of the foot and allowing another player to kick at it fairly hard. There is a considerable impact but no danger to the player who is blocking the ball. Care should be taken by the kicker, however, since he is likely to feel the greater discomfort.

3. As the tackle is made one of the players leans away from the ball. This causes the weight to be transferred away from the line of the tackle and force cannot be transmitted or held through the ball and against the opponent.

Plate 61

4. The tackler leans over the ball as the tackle is made. This is often the case with tall players. The player who has lowered his body and who applies tackling force from behind the ball is in a position to force the ball through his opponent's legs and his opponent is not in a position to resist.
5. The ankle is loose and partly extended. This is a weak position for the joint. When a block tackle is used the foot should be held firmly at right angles to the lower leg. This is the strongest position for the ankle since the muscles of the leg are strongly employed in holding the position.

SIDE BLOCK TACKLES (*plate* 61)

This tackle is usually required when an opponent is running away with the ball and the tackler is approaching him from behind. The principles of the front block tackle are employed but the tackler

COACHING AND TEACHING TECHNIQUES

must try to ensure that he is as close as possible to the ball before he commits himself. If possible the non tackling foot should be level with or slightly in front of the ball as the tackler pivots on it to bring himself into the block tackling position. The body will pivot quickly and powerfully on the standing foot in order to develop enough momentum to overcome or resist the running momentum of the player with the ball.

Common faults in side block tackling

1. The tackler commits himself to a tackle when he is behind the ball. This means that he has no possibility of transferring weight into the tackle. He is unable to pivot into the block tackling position.
2. The tackler attempts to stretch into the tackle which often results in him falling either as a result of the tackle being brushed aside or because he throws himself off balance by stretching.

As a player with the ball runs away from an opponent who he knows is trying to get into a tackling position, he will often transfer the ball to the foot which is furthest away from the tackler. This makes a block tackle extremely difficult if not impossible to execute. In these circumstances the tackler may have to use a sliding tackle.

SLIDING TACKLE

The sliding tackle is usually employed as a desperate measure to combat dangerous developments in attacking play. It is most frequently seen when an attacker has broken clear of the defence and is running towards goal with the ball. In these circumstances a defender may feel that if he takes the time necessary to get into a block tackling position his opponent may have been given enough time to take a shot at goal. In this situation the defender must prevent the shot by sliding the ball away to another defender or, more usually, out of play. When using a sliding tackle the defender will be on the ground and, therefore, should the tackle fail, he will be out of the game momentarily. It follows, therefore, that before committing himself to a sliding tackle, a player must be certain of success, or alternatively, the situation must be so dangerous that any attempt, however great the risk, must be made. Here are the ingredients of this method of tackling:

1. The tackler must be as near to his opponent as circumstances permit.
2. The tackling leg is the one furthest away from the opponent.

This means that the tackler goes to ground with his weight supported by the leg and thigh which he will use as his tackling leg.

3. The tackle is usually made after the opponent has played the ball forward or before he attempts to play it.
4. The tackler usually veers slightly away from his opponent before committing himself to the slide across the line of the ball's travel.

Since the tackling leg is in contact with the ground while it is stretched into the tackle there is little chance of injury occurring. In this technique the purpose of the tackle is to slide the ball away from an opponent. There is, however, also the possibility of sliding into a form of block tackle. In this technique the following points are worth noting:

1. The tackler must be close to the player with the ball.
2. As he prepares to go into the tackle the inside leg is doubled up and as the tackle begins the player takes his weight upon that leg and, often, the hand on that side of the body. The tackling (outside) leg is swung across as the tackler leans in towards his opponent and the inside of the foot is used to block the ball. Stability is maintained because the tackler is in the lowest possible position: on the ground. By the same token, should he make a slight error in judgement, the player is fully committed and out of the game.

Sliding tackles are rather desperate methods of challenging for the ball and entail risks. The main risk involves an error of judgement whereby the ball is missed and a defender is momentarily out of action. The second involves the possiblity of tripping an opponent which, in certain circumstances, can bring about exactly that which the tackle is designed to prevent, a goal being scored from a free kick or a penalty.

There are other methods of tackling which may be used by individual players but which, generally speaking, are less successful than those recommended previously.

TACKLING WITH THE HEEL

In this technique, where a player is running behind an opponent and attempting to tackle him, the heel tackle is made using the foot nearest to the opponent and can only be made when the opponent is controlling the ball with the foot which is nearest to the tackler. As the players are running along side by side, the tackler moves his tackling leg over the ball and blocks it with his heel as it touches the ground.

TACKLING WITH THE OUTSIDE OF THE FOOT

In the same position as for the heel tackle, the tackler's inside foot is used and the ball is blocked by turning the foot outwards as the opponent attempts to play the ball. The danger here is that the leg and ankle are in a weak position and if the player stumbles and falls there is the possibility of the tackler receiving a severe strain at the knee joint or even a fracture.

Tackling and struggling for possession of the ball is a vital and exciting part of soccer. Some players are well prepared by temperament to become strong tacklers. These are the aggressive players who are confident in their physical attributes. They are not necessarily big men but they are full of determination. This is not to say that some players are incapable of becoming effective tacklers. As a technique, tackling can be learned in exactly the same way as any other technique. Not everyone will become a tough, tenacious tackler but everyone can become better as it with intelligent coaching and practice.

CONCLUSIONS

There is no single answer to the problems involved in the development of skilful football. Wherever the game is played, skilful play depends upon the co-ordination of individual understanding. Players are individuals and they must be encouraged to progress as individuals. Good coaching accepts this and welcomes individuality while guiding it towards the best possible advance in team play. Poor coaching attempts to stereotype play and restrict players' imaginations. Restriction must lead to stagnation in the game. Football is not a mechanical exercise but an activity designed to provide limitless scope for creative ability. It is almost unique in the different and changing facets of its beauty and appeal. The precision of high speed combination, the sparkle of delicate dribbling, the soaring menace of the great header of a high ball, together with the probing intelligence of the player who can direct and dictate the course of a game—all play a part in the fascination of soccer. Power, artistry, speed, strength and skill combine to give the activity a compelling magnetism. Players and coaches must strive to find new techniques and ideas since standards are never absolute.

From time to time different aspects of the game appear to

dominate our considerations, perhaps, after a while, giving way to changed emphases. Defence may become the predominant factor until new concepts of attacking play challenge and overcome it. Teams assume an apparently permanent right to success until they fall into temporary decline and their successes fade into nostalgic memory. Will the game ever be the same again? Such is the dynamic nature of soccer that its adherents must exist in a semi-permanent state of dissatisfaction. Dissatisfaction is the forerunner of change. Change is a challenge to intelligence and inventiveness.

The game inevitably goes forward, often apparently by going backward, and if this book helps people to understand the inevitability of change then it has been worthwhile.